HEAD CASE

My Father, Alzheimer's & Other Brainstorms

ALEXIS ORGERA

Kore Press
Tucson
2021

Kore Press, Inc.
A Division of Kore Press Institute
325 West Second Street, #201
Tucson, AZ 85705
www.korepress.org

Cover and Interior design by Shanna Compton

We express gratitude to the Arizona Commission on the Arts, the Literary Arts Emergency Fund, and to individuals for support to make this Kore Press Institute publication possible.

ARIZONA
COMMISSION
ON THE **ARTS**

ISBN: 978-1-888553-81-9

Library of Congress Cataloging-in-Publication Data

Names: Orgera, Alexis, author.
Title: Head case : my father, Alzheimer's & other brain storms / Alexis
   Orgera.
Description: First edition. | Tucson : Kore Press, 2021.
Identifiers: LCCN 2021010407 | ISBN 9781888553819 (trade paperback)
Subjects: LCSH: Alzheimer's disease--Patients--Biography. |
   Brain--Diseases--Patients. | Father and child--Biography. | Alzheimer's
   disease--Patients--Family relationships. | Caregivers--Biography.
Classification: LCC RC523 .O74 2021 | DDC 616.8/3110092 [B]--dc23
LC record available at https://lccn.loc.gov/2021010407

This is a work of remembering, which inevitably
includes misremembering. And forgetting.

This book is dedicated to Mom, Ry, and Ken, and to Bo Dad, of course.

Contents

The mind is but a visitor:
It thinks us out of our world.
                    —Rainer Maria Rilke, *Book of Hours*

You are everywhere partial and entire
You are on the inside of everything and on the outside.
                    —A. R. Ammons, "Hymn"

YOUR LAST WORD

*. . . we were beginning, it seemed to me, to live our lives
in dissociated bits and pieces. The narrative spine of an
individual life was disappearing. The order of events was
becoming increasingly meaningless.*

—Barry Lopez, "Learning to See"

WHEN THE BRAIN decides it can no longer subsist on linear time, what's left is a series of pinpricks in space that say, *This is you. This is your story.* But those pockmarks delineate a failure: the dots don't connect. My father's last word became something of dire importance—the way things come together: a bullet to the brain, a sock to the eyeball. On NPR months before his death, an exiled writer: "Dictatorship by its very nature is only interested in one narrative." This is why writers and artists are exiled at all, providing alternatives to the autocrat, encouraging the masses to rise up against tyranny. Alzheimer's became, for us, a dictatorship of the mind with no space for relief or hope.[1] Tyranny doesn't see nuance. It can't hold us at three a.m. when we've been crying for days. It can't understand the tinkerer, the memory shark, the black suits of mourning, the dog's paw resting on the cat's head. One narrative: inside, outside, upside down.

---

[1]According to the Alzheimer's Association's 2019 report, 5.8 million Americans are living with Alzheimer's Disease. Roughly 200,000 of those people will be under 65, like Dad was—diagnosed at 52, dead by 60. By the

year 2050, an estimated 14 million people will have Alzheimer's disease. In 2019, Alzheimer's and other dementia care costs were $290 billion in the US. It's our country's sixth leading cause of death. Chances are somebody you know has or will have Alzheimer's. Maybe it will be you. Maybe it will be me.

When Dad died, we sent his brain off to a Miami research lab studying the brains of dementia patients. We got a report back that startled us. While he'd been diagnosed with Alzheimer's, in addition to the characteristic tangles and plaques in the brains of those with the disease, the researchers had found Lewy bodies and signs of vascular dementia. He'd been juggling at least three different diseases.

WE KEPT VIGIL around the clock for weeks. The hospice nurses had been sure he'd go at any moment, but every day his body defied them. He was sixty and still strong so that through the horse doses of morphine and the starvation, his zonked body held.

We left for two hours. I wanted Mom to have breakfast and a shower.

On our way back, we got the call. Dad had died.

This happens a lot—dying people wait until they're alone. Even when their brains are glue.

Mom wept and lay with his body for hours and hours. The rest of us barely breathed.

I know if I find you I will have to leave the earth . . .
And I know if I find you I will have to stay with the earth . . .
— A. R. Ammons, "Hymn"

DAD HAD A famous piece of advice: "Fuck 'em and feed 'em beans." I hope his last thought was a fuck you to Alzheimer's. It feels important that he closed his circle on earth with *something*. If he was trying to save us from that moment, from the sound of air being sucked out of the room as his breath ceased, I hope he made himself chuckle. If he wanted privacy when he met his maker, I hope his maker is a nimble trickster.

I think of him grinning—troublemaker glint in his blue eyes—all over the universe.

BLUEPRINTS, TIME'S WAVE, morning coffee, football sweats, pirate ship, people watcher, dinner prayer, sledgehammer, smell of sawdust, birth and death, claw hammer, white socks, deck shoes, church suit, sweat rings, yin and yang, Vanagon or minivan, altar boy, rock collector, gray hair, spider saver, death stare, even temper, wide-eyed photo pose, two-by-fours, crawl space, Chevy truck, sing off-key, quiet mumble, family man, fried bananas, cast iron pan, blowtorch, snake rake, riding mower, garden hoe, blue paint, last rights, sandpaper, righteous anger, capital letters, folded notes, waffle maker, donut getter, bricklayer, stranded boat, weekend fishing on the pier, swinging vines, sitting here, sitting together watching water.

NARRATIVE, FROM *gnarus*, knowing. He could visualize his way into and out of the myriad problems of building a house;

> he could draw in the air over morning coffee his theory of time as a wave crashing onto itself, wearing his twenty-year-old high school football sweats;

> he could build a pirate ship out of scraps—for a project I saved until the last minute;

> he liked to stare. We watched people together from car windows and park benches and imagined stories for their lives: the debonair pickpocket, the psychic five-year-old.

If a narrative imitates, it also creates.

Steinbeck's narrator in *East of Eden*: "I believe that there is one story in the world, and only one, that has frightened and inspired us, so that we live in a Pearl White serial of continuing thought and wonder."

Struggle between good and evil, ignorance and knowledge, yin and yang, birth and death. The myth of original sin. Narrative orbits the internal struggle between poles. Steinbeck: "A man, after he has brushed off the dust and chips of his life, will have left only the hard, clean questions: Was it good or was it evil? Have I done well—or ill?"

The final word.

Don't ask me how. I just showed up for the game.

—Dad

THE DUST AND chips: Work at six o'clock in the morning. A cup of weak coffee, then two. Work is two-by-fours, nails, sawhorses. Work smells like sawdust. Work is a crew of men who spackle and paint and lay carpet early before the 108-degree day comes to full swelter. Work is the oldies station blasting through a beat-up boom box. Work is a faded red Chevy pickup. Work is window casings, shingles. Work curls your fingers around a hammer and keeps them curled when you loosen your grip. Work is sod and piles of scrap lumber, errant screws and new bathtubs stained with grout.

What he hated most about Alzheimer's was his uselessness. *What am I supposed to do?* he asked. I tried to give him odd jobs: pulling up carpet staples so I could refinish the original heart pine at my house, raking leaves, painting walls every shade of ridiculous. For the first time in his life, he didn't finish what he started. I've always defined my father by his work ethic, and as his friends told me one summer before Dad was too far gone, and we were all gathered for a reunion in Connecticut, work was one of the defining features of his teenage years too. "It was football, and then it was all work after that," John tells me.[2]

---

[2]*Ron:*

It was the summer of 1970 or so, and I was working at Bloomingdale's that summer, and I thought I was working hard, but that particular day, I got up to go to work, and as I was leaving my house, who was coming up the driveway but Bo Orgera. And it was early in the morning, and he was working as a Stamford, Connecticut, garbage man. He marched right by me and picked up both of our family garbage cans, and he said, "Mornin' Ron," and he walked down the driveway, put the cans on the truck. I tried to talk to him, but he said, "I can't talk. I gotta get to the next house." I went to work and got out around midafternoon. I was driving down the street, and I looked over at a house near Bloomingdale's, and there's a guy in galoshes pumping out a house that was flooded. I looked more closely, and it was Bo Orgera. It was three in the afternoon, and Bo was pumping someone's basement. So I stopped the car and walked over.

I said, "I thought you were working the garbage."

"Nope, I'm pumping out a house," he said.

"How long will it take?"

"A couple hours. Then I have more houses to pump."

Later that night, my little sister Marcia asked me to take her to Dairy Queen, so I drove her to Dairy Queen, and when we walked in, who was behind the counter serving us Dairy Queen? Your father. I say, "Bo?"

He says, "Yeah, what would you like?"

John:
[During the summer of 1973, Dad and John worked for a man named Murray at a demolishing company.]

This one particular summer, Murray sent us to Orange, Connecticut, to a place called Yale Transportation, a trucking company. They were taking down the trucking depot building. The first day on the job, they gave us each a two-sided axe with a big handle, and we climbed up onto the building. It's a flat roof, all gravel, and a layer of asbestos, I think it was, and then sheet metal, and so you're trying to chop through pebbles on this roof with a two-bladed axe to make a path and then roll up all this gobbledy-gook and get it off the roof in an area the size of a football field. I figured we'd never be able to get this done. I look over and there's Bo, and he's got the first strip done already, and he's looking at me like, "Well, come on, are you gonna get to work or what?"

Joe:

I was a good athlete, but in my household my rebellion was accepted, maybe even encouraged a little bit, so when I found my coaches to be as-sholes, I rebelled. Your father never rebelled. He took it all and said, *this is my job, this is my responsibility.* In some cases that's good, but we come to find now, in 2012, maybe not so good after all.

Peter:

I was a New York Jewish intellectual type. Bo was a football star, and he was good with his hands. I've never thought of myself as smarter than Bo, just different. Your father could do things I could never do—engineering, drafting, mathematical things. In a million years I could never do what he did. He was our leader because he could do everything better. He always had more money in his pocket—he had all these different jobs. Your family had the connections for all the jobs.

In an Omaha people's creation story called "The Flaming Rock," a giant rock rose up suddenly out of the flooded Earth and burst into flames. Those flames triggered evaporation and created landmasses where fruit trees and grasses grew abundantly. During this time, spirit beings had been looking for a place to settle. They'd tried the uninhabitable sun and moon. They'd even tried Earth, but there had been nowhere to land, to settle into physical form, before the flaming rock. Finally, the spirit beings could live on Earth as corporeal beings, and they were grateful.

In contrast, as the brain shrivels, its fluid-filled ventricles expand and multiply until the skull's a series of interconnected, polluted swimming pools—water and fire on two ends of a pocked battlefield. In the Alzheimer's brain, collaboration between the elements becomes impossible. In the mind's final frontiers, Dad lost both motor skill and memory as the disease spread from cerebrum to cerebellum—the how-to-fix-the-object along with the name of the object itself; the location of the sock drawer and the purpose of a sock. At the end of the tunnel, mere sitting and making Os with his mouth, staring with the bluest eyes, and finally loss of all physical and mental continence. Finally, deep drool fields. I've seen it in old men, and I watched it in my middle-aged father.

AND THEN, THE Tree of Knowledge beckoning, original sin, the generational ticking clock. Sins of the fathers: Cain and Abel making good on their parents' foibles. But mythology wants more from the garden as progenitor of original sin. Mythos wants explanations for life and death, the revealed secret. It wants Adam and Eve to represent two hemispheres of one brain: the paths we take that make us human. It wants epigenetics: original trauma wrapped in methyl groups like fists around our DNA so that all experience is one, all suffering connected. The genetic origins for sins of the father. It still wants symbolic fruit: that round orb of the rose family, the downfall of woman, the sex-organ stand-in, the doctor's hex bag—apple as the object of choice. It's awash in domestic futures: feminine swallow and masculine prod vying for a place at the dinner table: how we create each other, how we map our stories.

During Alzheimer's, Dad began to eat apples whole, core and all. Lost his protocol. In French, there's apple and apple-of-the-earth, roundness abounds. Not all apples are cultivated. Some are wild. Some have never been tamed. Some ride as undetected witches in the night sky. Some put Snow Whites to sleep. Apples carry us away. Banish us. Seedlings become our flesh cart. Sweet, wild fruit of the Kazakhstan forests bisected by the Silk Road. Apple, as in throttle, as in joyous mole, as in perpetual motion machine.

Apple
Kingdom: Plantae   Order: Rosales
Family: Rosaceae   Subfamily: Amygdaloideae   Genus: Malus
Species: *M. domestica*

The scientific landscape is code: apple, a plant with rosy blood (Rosales), with a skin rash (Rosaceae), conducting emotions via its own fibrous nature (Amygdaloideae), with many unpleasant circumstances to circumscribe it (Malus). A faulty domesticity (*M. domestica*). Maladjusted heart. Mal du siècle: always carrying the weariness of the world in a cavernous bite mark. *Mala fide*: with the intent to deceive. Like any good fall from innocence, we're rooted in the *Malus domestica*, but only so much as language makes it so.

MARIA AND DANTE'S[3] house was surrounded by woods full of wild blueberries, vegetable gardens and grape vines, gooseberries, mulberry trees, plum trees, chestnuts, apple trees, cherry trees. At Bette and Tony's, a vegetable garden, winding vines of scuppernongs, my favorite fruit, and figs. Entire afternoons gorging in gardens. When you're a kid you consume until someone tells you not to. Plenty of summers nobody told me to stop. If the myth of Adam and Eve had included a child in the garden, she'd have eaten every apple on that Tree of Knowledge without guilt.

We ate baked apples in Maria and Dante's kitchen, skins and all, mashed into applesauce. In that kitchen, too, Nonno and I made *zuppona*, a breakfast gruel of warm milk and stale bread, coffee for color: *big soup* in English. We slurped chicken broth with tiny stars. "Faccio un po' di brodo," Nonna would offer as the designated maker of healing broths. In Bette and Tony's kitchen: late night snacks of white bread and butter, homemade bread-and-butter pickles in huge jars, peanut butter cookies fresh out of the oven.

As a kid, I could sample without guilt or fear. I could eat the apple core, too, if I wanted. That's the funny thing about a disease like Alzheimer's. It takes you back to childhood before it erases you altogether.

---

[3]My maternal grandparents are Maria (Nonna) and Dante (Nonno). My paternal grandparents are Bette (Gramma Bette) and Tony (Poppy).

ARISTOTLE's *hamartia*, the fatal flaw, the sin or fault of living. The choice that leads to downfall. On a deathbed you must define your narrative. The how-did-I-live-narrative. A body asks, *Did I do this well?* A photo above my writing desk torn from a magazine portrays a silver-haired woman wearing plastic boots, holding a trowel on the rooftop of a city garden.

I want to be her when I'm old.

As a kid, I'd squeeze my eyes shut and envision the world as a giant egg floating through space; we, passengers on a smooth monolith.

I THREW UP twice in the bushes by the pond. Sprawled on my back on a picnic table, wearing Mom's parachute shirt bursting with yellow and black flowers, I was flanked by two church men. The sunlight killed my head. The men geared up to pray over me. Well-meaning, thick-fingered southern farmers, a father-and-son elder and deacon combo, their hands mitted my face and head as my parents stood by watching. One of them pulled a small square cloth from a white business-sized envelope, a tiny miracle anointing cloth. "Dear Lord," they prayed, "send the spirit of infirmity away from this child."

If only it were so simple to banish migraine from the garden, linked and intertwined as it is to all the other plants and animals therein. Migraine's my trickster, my four-legged snake. Those men prayed with their eyes squeezed shut, and they believed. Eighty or so church members fumbled under a picnic shelter nearby, trying not to stare; church ladies prepped the meal—seventeen varieties of deviled egg including purple pickled quail eggs—church men sat in clumps, kids steered clear of my sick-self, playing on the other side of the park. I became the spectacle. The lesson. The symbol. I was possessed by my own brain reactions and desperate for a spirit world to release me.

Define your narrative before obliteration. At twelve, during a church picnic, migraine had been my narrative for eight years already.

TEXT IS THE amalgamation, the horse glue, of passed-down story line. Political power in the way a story is told, how terms are defined. The Book of Acts: apostles roam the countryside preaching to and converting the masses. In chapter sixteen they meet up with an enslaved woman who makes money for her owners through divination. When she finds the apostles, she follows them for days, calling out incessantly, "These men are servants of the Most High God, who are telling you the way to be saved."

Paul gets annoyed with the woman's noise. To silence her, he proclaims she's demon possessed. To silence her is to remove her mythmaking power. Take away the handiwork of god-or-devil and what do we have but ourselves, our own responsibility to ourselves?

My demon is a foghorn, a gray scream. It's made of my DNA and a strung web of cerebral complexities. Demon possession is a good scapegoat, it is *the* scapegoat. The thing that needs removing in order to feel catharsis.

Narrative is an escape artist. What is exorcism if not mirror-loathing?

In Brigit Pegeen Kelly's poem "Song," the narrative of a girl's pet goat, stolen and murdered by group of teenage boys. The poem hinges on this narrative thread, but the song that a dead goat sings, its final echo, one that penetrates, repeats, and reverberates in the landscape is the poem's catharsis. In this way, the narrative is both secondary to and an integral part of the poem's connective tissue. It's first line commands: "Listen: there was a goat's head hanging by ropes in a tree." Jostling between song and silence. "And those who heard it / Felt a hurt in their hearts and thought they were hearing / The song of a night bird." What we hear, the goat's song, is the lasting memory of the poem. Final words are important, the crescendo of that last song enters the boys:

> What they didn't know
> Was that the goat's head would go on singing, just for them,
> Long after the ropes were down, and that they would learn to listen . . .

THE *anagnorisis*: to see the truth of a situation. Story as distinct from plot. Middle words: bombs today, earthquakes tomorrow, decrepitude always. War stories predicated on violence; in her poem "Spelling," Margaret Atwood recounts the story of a pregnant woman in a war whose thighs are tied together so she can't give birth.

Poppy, a medic in the war. His brother, my great-uncle, was General Patton's wartime dentist. Both among the first wave of soldiers to set foot on Normandy on D-Day. But what does this tell you? Nothing about the relationship between brothers, the blame and guilt around their mother's untimely death that shaped their entire lives, and probably Dad's too.

Nonna lived under an apple tree in Italy for three weeks while the Americans bombed her German-occupied city. "Under an apple tree," I think, is code for "in the country": she left her town with her sisters and mother to live in the country during the bombings. Before they left, she'd helped to hide young women under floorboards, under the voices of big, blond German soldiers. As she tells it, she was too young at fifteen to be counted among the rape-spoils. No story is ever true.

Nonno spent three years in a British POW camp in northern Africa, not far from Tripoli. He wrote of fellow prisoners, "I saw men making mandolins, wooden artifacts of all kinds. Guys unraveling woolen socks into a ball and using the threads to make sweaters, using hooked needles made out of old clothes hangers. Someone making teeth out of ivory, cigarette lighters out of aluminum pieces, using shards of glass and razor blades to scrape the metal into shape." He was put in charge of vehicle maintenance in the camp, MacGyvered lamps for the barracks from spare wire and truck engines, learned English, and ate a daily stew of desert sand.

After the war, when he put down his fork, he'd say, "Always leave the table hungry."

THEN, THE *peripeteia*. Turn around. Reversal. Which way will it run? Life moves along an axis until the axial fault line ruptures in another illness narrative to make sense of. Chaos narrative, never to return. I walk away from my original garden into my father's and his father's. What happens in the clouded mind? A grand Joseph Cornell collage of disparate parts where accreted bedlam equals beauty. When Dad said, "I don't know," over and over during his disease, he meant it more than any of us. Can you have a narrative if you've been stripped of memory?

Another uncle, Fred, was shot down above Germany in World War II. In the woods, snow all around, a young girl saves Fred, feeds him a peanut butter sandwich, and he lives. The story changes. Uncle Fred saved by nuns. No, he saves a little girl. No, he is captured. No, they hide him. Dad's fantastic iterations: the snow, the bare feet, no, the boots. When he told these variations, his lips quivered. The telling as poignant as salvation. He'd soon lose that story too. His mixed-up narratives frightened him. In the midst of wild frustration he said to me, "Why don't you just put me away somewhere. Please." Would he regress just enough to reach back and grab his first word away from its chewing mouth, his final word mirroring his first?

IMPORTANT EPISTEMOLOGICAL QUESTIONS: what is the story, and who's in charge? In the beginning, yes, was the word, and the *was* was with us, and the word was us. Everything is a revision. In the narrative of punishment, a slipping into pre-Christian polytheism, when God doles out his judgments for eating from the Tree of Knowledge in Genesis 3:22: *Behold, the man has become like one of Us,* says God. Then God kicks his human creations out of the garden, *lest he put out his hand and take also of the tree of life, and eat, and live forever.* In this narrative—the one written but conveniently overlooked—God is afraid of humans becoming gods so he plays petulant judge and jury: Eve will let her husband rule over her; Adam will struggle with barren land/ desert sand.

When I was a kid, demons hid in my closet, and the snake in the garden was the thing to fear, but in the story on the page, the snake is simply a trickster setting events into motion, the metahistory a series of vastly myriad interpretations. The master narrative, when protected as such, becomes a dictatorship of the mind, so maybe losing one's plot ain't so bad, Dad. In the beginning, some words.

THE PERFECTIONIST ME can find ways to explain the world, but they're seldom true: fixed surfaces are defined by intractability. I still don't know, for instance—despite facts and figures, reason and logic—if migraine created my demons or if my imagination (as Joan Didion writes in her essay "In Bed") created migraine (and demon). But I do know what Alzheimer's does: it turns the hallucinatory into reality. In a brain full of billions of neurons, things go wrong. One bundle of electricity communicates all sorts of catastrophes. When a migraineur's serotonin receptors go awry, blood vessels flair into sunbursts. Nothing is solid or anchored as it should be, but it's temporary mayhem. A neuron can morph into a lamp for the old performances of dust on the church podium; or hide along the riverbanks where a minor character from childhood drowned and sunk into my skull; or carve a pathway for voicing over an apocalyptic slideshow to the tune of "We Didn't Start the Fire" in front of the entire seventh grade. In my world, neuron can play god. In Dad's world, god got lost in tangles and plaques.

NARRATIVE, TO RECOUNT, from *narrare*, from *gnarus*. Full circle. When a sparkling thing happens, you want to tell someone, to embellish and ornament the day-to-day. A nightmare always wants recounting in the morning. Out of nostalgia, childhood wants recollection, even the memories that aren't real, the imaginary birds and dream injuries. History and myth too:

At six, horrified, I narrated the Saint Andrews Christmas play, in charge of my group's telling. Standing on a box in my navy and white uniform, I recounted the story of the Christ child and his virgin mom, and his lambs, and his hay.

Narrative is a story or part of a story.

Two years later, my parents swore off Catholicism and its graven images, its idols, its stories. Quest narrative is something found, some hurdle jumped. My parents fell deep and headlong into the mothwing pages of the New King James Bible with its lockbox blue concordance on every coffee table of my memory; they sought-and-found a Truth with all its wrong turns, one-way roads.

Not long after we moved to South Carolina, there had been a woman named Athena—platinum cloud of hair, gold bathing suit, and gold heeled sandals—straight out of myth, their poolside Carolina spirit guide. When Athena proved to be a fraud who just wanted to be paid for the Truth, then came the Worldwide Church of God with its rented bingo hall church services, and nothing that resembled the familiar, hovering in a swamp of backwater. There are a few things you can't strip narrative away from, memory being alive, transferable.

IN THE HOT afterglow of burning cities, wrapped in a lamb's wool tunic, Edith turned and looked at her home, Sodom and Gomorrah, the narrow streets she'd strolled with her infant daughters, on which she'd bought olives and oils. The pain in her heart was a crevasse, so she gave that nearly imperceptible sign to her god, a sweet/sad tilt of the head, a whispered yes, that nobody saw or heard—not Lot or the daughters he'd offered up as sacrificial lambs to the angry townspeople to "do to them whatever you like," in exchange for those supposed angels—and her god, out of compassion, complied.

Edith the memory bunker, salt-temple arm of the breathing desert.

Edith the ultimate.

Her final word was *yes*, was *please*.

DAD'S LAST DAYS were punctuated by a weird crab walk on the floor of his urine-stained room; his head swollen from ramming himself into walls. Worse than a burning city, he'd become an invading alien begging for obliteration. For yes. For please.

A brick wall erects itself in my body.

In the courtyard of the facility, he loved to sit in direct sunlight. He'd raise is face to the sky, eyes closed, and smile. Out in the sun with him, I imagined the palettes of color that recreated the past. I read him poems, and he smiled. From Yusef Komunyakaa's "My Father's Love Letters": "The gleam of a five-pound wedge / On the concrete floor / Pulled a sunset / through the doorway of his toolshed."

In the poem, the speaker's father—a carpenter—attempts to write love letters to his estranged wife, whom he abused, and the son helps the father write these letters. The poem finds a moment of tenderness, even as its context has already battered the hell out of wife and, presumably, son. In the end:

> This man,
> Who stole roses & hyacinth
> For his yard, would stand there
> With eyes closed & fists balled,
> Laboring over a simple word, almost
> Redeemed by what he tried to say.

IN THE PROPER hands, our disparate narratives can connect us. My parents' journey marks me, a story maelstromed onto my skin. We are all seekers, it says. A poet friend writes: "I still believe—however naïvely—that poems can speak to other human beings and can make collective society consider our own convictions, experiences, and beliefs." Poems are the opposite of dictators. Why is it naïve to want to get inside the chest of another person? To want to live there inside someone's ribcage, inside words garbled and glistening like a child's first syllabics? After all, there's no slipshod, broke-down *memoria technica* that can separate my timeline from Dad's. We're a dance. We're a wind dance, a sun dance, a loosed thread dancing in the clouds.

Is a narrative unmasked a narrative at all? Mythology transforms into the reality of lived experience. Stephen Dobyns on writing: "What will bear the burden of all that noise?" The scream of living, its linearity or chaos, passes into bell into loudspeaker into canyon echo. So cacophonous, there must be just one word that we repeat over and over to drown it out. With throat on fire I remember Atwood's poem: "How do you learn to spell?" she writes, "Blood, sky & the sun, / your own name first, / your first naming, your first name, / your first word."

Your first utterance and—looking back, being forced to look back—maybe your last.

PHOTOGRAPH

Photography is an elegiac art, a twilight art. Most subjects photographed are, just by virtue of being photographed, touched with pathos.

—Susan Sontag, *On Photography*

IN THE PHOTO of us at the apartment complex pool, we're characters in our own light show. The sun, low slung and unseen in the sky, casts a diffuse lemon light into and through Dad's white shirt, as though his torso is lit from the inside. He slants his head toward the camera. He's outlined in a pencil stroke of sunlight that radiates in fine tendrils through the loose white parts of his button-down shirt. His mouth opened just a little in half smile, half smirk. Eyes squint behind eighties eyeglasses. The hazy outlines of trees behind us mask what I knew was beyond them: a ditch replete with tadpoles, red clay, and trickling water—where I'd spend many hours of my childhood collecting treasures—and beyond that an off-limits golf course where teenagers drank and made out at night.

Light and shadow play over the photographic world.

HERE AND EVERYWHERE

Dr. Alzheimer: How are you?
Auguste D.: It was quite good the last few days.
Dr. Alzheimer: Where are you?
Auguste D.: Here and everywhere—here and now—you mustn't take offense."[4]

WHERE ARE YOU? Where are *you*? Molecule after molecule bursts into form in a series of finite points that curve into our body-lines. Cells call place names to other cells over a bridge of synapse so that we become shapes both earthbound and transcendent. Such an answerable question: Where are you? *Here* and *here*, then *there* and *there*. I attempt to both map and obliterate memory against a backdrop of grief. Searching for meaning: every moment is now. A perfect future is our goal: the hope of fleeing the burning city. Logic tells us we exist only in one place at a time, no escape except through our own movement. Quantum theory has demonstrated that the same atom can appear in two places at once: if I'm here, I might also be there.

---

[4]Interview transcripts and biographical information about Auguste Deter and Dr. Alzheimer are from *Alzheimer: The Life of a Physician & the Career of a Disease* by Konrad and Ulrike Maurer, though I have imagined some of Auguste's interior and exterior world.

I ran across another version of the translation of "you mustn't take offense" somewhere on the internet, which was "you don't mind."

I AM HERE making a story: in bed for weeks, I'd lost track of time. A nervous breakdown is full of dark holes, caves, hallucinatory dreams, racing hearts, and this was doozy of a breakdown. Sometimes in order to be able to get out of bed in the morning, you just keep moving like a shark. Until you can't, and you stop. Still, there we were in the midst of it a year to the day after Dad died: three generations of women sprinkling his ashes into the creek, into wide Florida sky, into the Bermuda grass behind the house. Nonna sang in Latin from a Catholic death mass. Mom and I grabbed clumps of him and threw him into the air.

"He'll be fish food," Mom said. We followed an imaginary arc of Dad's ashes across the earth from the backwaters of our creek out to the Gulf of Mexico with a jumping mullet, into the sharp beak of an osprey and so on out into the universe. We laughed. We cried. For a few moments we saw him everywhere. The dust of him glanced over the pine trees and mangroves.

SEARCH FOR IMAGES of the first named patient with Alzheimer's Disease online and find a recurring photograph, in various stages of coloration and desaturation, of a woman who has *undergone*. In the photo, Auguste D. looks away from the camera toward the floor, or whatever visions the floor presents her. Her eyes are almond shaped, murky ponds—by turns empty and seeking—weighted with sandbags. The lines on her face, especially on her forehead, dig dust-bowl deep, tilled with anxiety as unwatered rows of farmland. Her skin is tanned and weathered. Her shoulder-length hair's matted and variously disheveled, partly pinned, partly flopping to her shoulder. Thick, masculine fingers clasp each other just above her knees, fingernails dirty, where her legs are drawn up into a soiled hospital gown with tiny, translucent buttons running down its front. She's been captured and memorialized. On November 29, 1901, Dr. Alzheimer asked her to write her name. Instead, she wrote only "Mrs." and repeated, "I have, so to speak, lost myself."

I AM HERE: in creative writing class I shared Aimee Bender's very short story, "The Rememberer" with my students. It's a story in which the main character laments her lover's reverse evolution (loss of self). The lover, Ben, turns into an ape after denouncing the human condition: brains that grow huge, disproportionately, compared to our hearts. He regresses from ape all the way down to "one-celled wonder, bloated and blind, brainless, benign, heading clear and small like an eye-floater into nothingness." Bender's narrator muses on her fear of total loss—her limits discovered in the fear of the total annihilation of a lover.

Which is exactly what happens in real life, life outside of the metaphor of this story, I mean, to all the witnesses of a disease like Alzheimer's. You watch helplessly as the person loses everything. We ask and we ask, like Bender's narrator asks her lover, "Do you remember me? Do you remember?" even as the brain-sick person fades right before our eyes. And why is it so important that we be remembered?

Auguste D.: I don't feel like it and I don't have time.
Dr. Alzheimer: For what?
Auguste D.: I would very much like to ask myself that.

To LOSE IS to misplace your story in the trenches. A body without a soul. An automaton without mythos. Time passes, loss. A walk in an unfamiliar woods. When a loved one dies loss feels like a hunk of flesh taken. A person to miss, a missing person. Power loss during a thunderstorm. Lost ship. Win/loss percentages in games and wars. From the Old English *los*, meaning destruction. Loss of self, in every sense slaughter. *Annus horribilis*: the year of misfortune.

Loss has many faces. In her poem "One Art" Elizabeth Bishop writes: "—Even losing you (the joking voice, a gesture / I love) I shan't have lied. It's evident / the art of losing's not too hard to master / though it may look like (*Write* it!) like disaster." But the reader knows, has known from the beginning, that loss is the hardest experience to master. How can we master the void? The eternal hole? The nothing that blooms from loss?

I am here making my story: I rifled through my shoebox of old photos. I pulled one out and asked, "Do you remember when I lived in California? You came to visit for holidays sometimes?" Blank stare. Unmarked grave. "No, no I don't," he said.

In the photo, a turkey nearly as big as the folding table we sat around. My parents, my sister, my ex-husband. A shotgun guest-house in Santa Monica Canyon just blocks from the Pacific where J— and I wrote and dreamed, rudderless and afraid, free, invincible, and us-against-the-world.

"Oh yes, you were over there in that place." *That place*, the better part of five years, a drop in the dementia bucket. California is my story not his.

That place, a missing piece for Dad, is the junction I've mapped between each of my cells, a gap across which impulses pass until I'm a whole body of cellular reminiscence. My first real taste of freedom: U-Haul cresting I-10 as we ascended a hill to overlook downtown LA—Beemers and the Staples Center, smog and more traffic than I'd ever seen: highways looping and crisscrossing over and under and around, convergences and traffic patterns, the twenty-four-hour rush hour that is Los Angeles. Then further west, the way sage and chaparral and eucalyptus perfumed the coastal air. A block from the ocean, the Pacific's waves pulsed over a desert of beach late at night; mornings were sea layers; evenings, fog. I was green, twenty-two, full of terror-wonder.

Of surfing in northern California Daniel Duane writes, "I thought again about throwing language all over a scene, wondered if the emotional mystery of one's response to place doesn't lie in the inchoate play of *possible* words, of felt meanings and poetries." Driving west, I had chosen possibility; I left my past in another time zone, on another wave where Dad would eternally expound on his old time-wave theories, to start a new story line, which is really a continuation of the old story line.

EARLY IN AUGUSTE'S stay at the Frankfurt asylum where she'd die, when Dr. Alzheimer asked her again where she was, and she answered, "At the moment; I have temporarily, as said, I don't have means. One has to just—I don't know myself—I don't know at all—," was she aware of her own decline, her last days representing a split in her own psyche like a personal BC to AD? Had she been a happy housewife? A contented mother? Did she have hobbies? Friends? Or was she trapped in her apartment cooking meals, cleaning, taking care of other people? Maybe she went for walks around her neighborhood with her little girl in tow, on snowy winter mornings, and maybe later when she found herself alone, she visited an elderly neighbor.

"The woman lives on the same corridor," Auguste said in one of the interviews, yelling the woman's name: "Mrs. Hensler, Mrs. Hensler, Mrs. Hensler." Maybe they shared a cup of strong tea, reminisced about a youth that slips by. Where was she then?

The first hints of something odd, from Maurer and Maurer:

"According to her husband's statement, Auguste D. had been quite normal until March 1901. On March 18, 1901, she suddenly claimed that he had gone for a walk with a female neighbor. This completely groundless assertion was the first thing that struck him. From that moment on Auguste had been full of mistrust about him and this neighbor. Shortly thereafter the husband noted a decline in her memory. Two months later, in May, she made obvious mistakes in food preparation for the first time and became restless, wandering aimlessly through the apartment. She increasingly neglected her housework; her condition deteriorated more and more. She then claimed 'constantly' that a carter, who often came into the house, wanted somehow to harm her."

Left to her own devices while her husband was at work, Auguste D. unraveled.

I AM HERE, too: After Dad unraveled into the air, so did I, though not irretrievably. Unravel, as in woven material: a sweater, a blanket. Unspool, as in fresh thread. Unfurl, into the green and living world. Penelope keeping her suitors at bay with the promise of completion. Every night, she unravels just a bit of her father-in-law's burial shroud, every morning she is free not to choose another husband as she bides her time. Unraveling is a shadow of choice. My unraveling: unplanned, a naked body calling out to the gods.

AUGUSTE DETER WAS fifty-six when she died in 1906, at which time her disease was still unnamed. Dr. Alzheimer suspected that Auguste wasn't suffering from the typical senile dementia—she was so young!—but he couldn't know it for sure until he later examined her postmortem brain. In a lecture in Tübingen after the autopsy, Dr. Alzheimer explained that he'd found spread over her cortex, "millet seed-sized lesions, which are characterized by the deposit of a peculiar substance in the cerebral cortex." What he'd found were plaques and decimated synapses in her brain. By chance or fortune, this wife of a railway clerk and mother of a grown daughter, would be the first-ever patient diagnosed with Alzheimer's Disease, though neither patient nor doctor could know how significant their meeting would become—or how prevalent her brain's masses of tangle and plaque as a phenomenon of decay.

When I began searching for photos of Auguste I needed to memorize her expression; I needed to know what to expect as Dad rammed his head full throttle into the end of the road like a man trapped in a burning race car. It was her eyes that illuminated the disease for me, the vacuum and mystery of them. Dad was fifty-eight, six years into the symptoms of dementia, when I began searching for her.

I AM HERE: Breaking up with J— in my fort in the closet, wearing a green clay facial mask. It's hard to write about J— even now as separate from myself. We *were* each other's twenties, woven into the fabric of each other—and we loved each other deeply.

I am also here: I met B— the year after we moved back to Florida; we took long walks along the Bay, and he named all the native trees and flowers.

I was a caged animal.

I AM HERE: at the funeral.

I AM HERE: fixing up my house to sell. Buying a camper in which to travel around the country.

I AM HERE: left in the Vermont woods. B— said he had no more empathy for my grief.

I AM HERE: at the writers' retreat, breathing underwater, drugged, objects in my periphery floating through space.

I AM HERE: in my sister Kendal's childhood bed, in my parents' house, Maria feeding me bits of boiled chicken with her fingers.

AUGUSTE D. TELLS us, *I am here. I am everywhere. I am here and now* as she unshackles all notions of time. In the command for her listener, *You mustn't take offense,* she asks that we not be bothered that she's transformed to condensation and evaporation recycled in an infinite, far-reaching rise and fall of breath. In the asylum, pieces of her selfhood flaked away like radioactive decay. She became a galaxy just too distant to see with any precision and moving further and further from the naked eye every moment—an outline in a hot-air balloon. During her last days, Auguste slept in her hospital bed as if it were a messy nest, her sheets curled and twisted around the protective comma of her body. Or she didn't sleep and was submerged in baths for hours and hours at a time. She screamed or muttered. She pissed and shat all over herself. She drooled and moaned, or she didn't drool and didn't moan. She became a skin bag and a bones bag. And then an explosion so powerful that she flew into a billion particulates of dust.

PHOTOGRAPH

Ultimately, having an experience becomes identical with taking a photograph of it.

—Sontag

As if through a window, I watch the photograph stuck to my desk, where Dad and I posed thirty-five years ago in the dying light beside our apartment complex pool. I see the water behind us, reflections of white and dark blue spooning each other in half-moon crags and shards on the water's surface. The reflections of trees are a frantic EKG. I see the deep-end mark, a black tile 8 licked by chlorine. The photo has composition by mistake, the fence line creating depth, the flower barrel behind his left arm, the deck slats pointing the viewer's eye toward the pool and reflecting sunlight onto Dad's back.

But me, I'm protected from the glare. I'm shaded and sheltered by Dad's body. I'm not looking at the camera, rather down and away to my left, my head resting on his torso. I'm not looking at anything at all: my congenital disappointment, the far-off stare that accompanies it. My arms hang limp at my sides; I'm wearing a delicate, thin, white short-sleeved dress shirt. Though the photo doesn't show them, I remember the shirt's eyelet accents.

Composition defines us. Out of the silence, there we are.

I have my own memories of this place, things Dad couldn't know: in this pool, as a preteen, the first boy to rub his hard penis against my body. We hovered in the deep end, he against the wall, me treading water. Our bodies touched and then repelled each other, as if sparring. My bony knees thumped his ribs. His wet hair flopped in fisty curls over one of his eyes. He had a gap in his front teeth, like me. He was cool, unlike me, but we were both still-awkward almost-teens, touching and not touching, feeling pinpricks against each other's bodies. He pulled me toward him. I grabbed onto the wall behind him. Other smaller kids played in the shallow end. He wrapped his boy legs around my torso, and that's when I felt him small and hard against my pelvic bone. We might have kissed, I don't re-member. He's nameless, an aqueous, brief encounter. But here in the photo taken years before, the pool casts a shadow of yin and yang as we pose at its lip.

A LANGUAGE WE HAVE YET TO DISCOVER

Dr. Alzheimer: What is your husband's name?
Auguste D.: I don't know . . .
Dr. Alzheimer: What name does your husband have?
Auguste D.: My husband isn't here right now.

. . .

Dr. Alzheimer: Do you have children?
Auguste D.: Yes, a daughter.
Dr. Alzheimer: What is her name?
Auguste D.: Thekla!

I'M THREE AGAIN, I'm dancing, I'm dancing naked in the bathroom lit by a red lampshade. Is it really red? Mom's filling the tub for a bath. She's kneeling on the floor. She's kneeling and singing to me. Mom's filling the tub for a bath. She's filling the tub. In the tub is water, and it makes sound. In my memory, the sound of water spilling. The room's lit in reds and yellows. Is it a yellow lampshade? I'm naked. The bathtub's running, and it's running in the next room and the next. Here's the mounted pencil sharpener below a light switch, the kind of sharpener in elementary school. In this mind-photograph I see myself naked; I stick my pinky into one of the sharpener's pencil holes and sharpen in the slosh of running water, the tear of grinding finger. The bell curve reveals a relationship between forgetting and time, but where is the curve for dream-as-memory? Does dream inhabit everywhere too? This memory scythes a mad C onto my synapses. The one thing, Emerson writes in his essay "Circles," "we seek with insatiable desire is to forget ourselves, to be surprised out of our propriety, to lose our sempiternal memory and to do something without knowing how or why; in short to draw a new circle." To seek is to be loosed from the restraints of reality, set loose as if on the heel of the first wheel.

ART MAKING BECOMES its own language, a way to comprehend and apprehend the world. The imagined world, when imagined well, speaks truth into the void. Dad and I painted and drew together every Wednesday. I thought art would be relaxing for him.

Over a period of months, Dad penciled hundreds of thumb-print-sized, broken circles into the pages of a legal pad. An act of obsession or devil's possession in the starburst of decline: circles in rows, circles with diagonals and zigzags connecting them, a planetary map. Circles growing strands of hair, like nerve cells buffered by synapse or weird cancer cells. Lines from a straight edge. Xs and Os in a deranged game of tic-tac-toe.

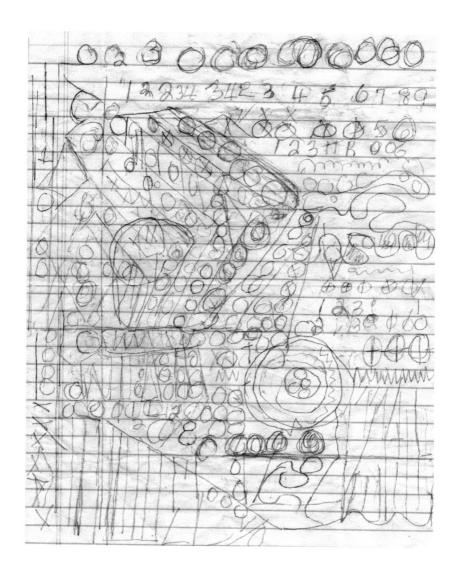

DAYS SHIFT AND fasten themselves onto better days or worse days like doors on rusty hinges. Auguste D. died within four and a half years of her first symptom. Some people live ten, twenty years inside the maze. On a scale of forgetting, sometimes I was his friend, most days I was a *nice girl,* occasionally his daughter, and sometimes a shadow-wife, Mom and I resembling two eras of the same woman. When he stared at me, told me I was pretty, I dreaded the possibility of his tongue shoving into my mouth. I pulled out photos of Mom and me in different eras. The one of Mom and Dad posing at their 70s wedding. The flecked photo of Mom pregnant with me, her hair pixie short, the photo's imperfections giving her freckles. The one of me, bucktoothed and boyish, at school. Or the one of me in glasses too big for my face, a stupid haircut. See, Dad, see how alike but different we are?

Emerson writes, "The man finishes his story,—how good! how final! how it puts a new face on all things. He fills the sky. Lo! on the other side rises also a man and draws a circle around the circle we had just pronounced the outline of the sphere," where we are overlapping concentric circles echoing ovoid sound, ripples on a pond before definition. Where experience follows experience based on collective memory.

MY 1961 EDITION of *Childcraft* encyclopedia, volume two, smells sweet like Easter bread. The first page of my favorite volume's lined with my kid scrawl—Xs and Os. Two parallel lines, then seven rows of Xs in three columns, another set of parallel lines with a rounded tip populated inside by Os, then another set of Xs in seven rows and three columns. It looks like a schematic for stadium seating. On page nineteen, my favorite illustration accompanies Vachel Lindsay's "Yet Gentle Will the Griffin Be." A cream-colored griffin with wide, white eyes and a pink tongue licking the Milky Way floats out of the egg-cracked and cratered, cream-colored moon. Below the hatched moon, a little boy in purple pajamas rearranges stars in the sky. From the boy's head, I've drawn three rays in pen, and above that in pencil I've drawn a circle with squiggles bounding from it. I've connected the universe.

THE CONCEPTUAL OPERATION of turning a system around an axis. *Don't fuck up the rotation: Puff puff give.* Rotate your crops. Plant. Fell. Replant. Curl curl curl. *Around around the mulberry bush so early in the morning. Round here he's slipping through my hands.* Planetary movement. A passage of privilege. A baton. That sneaky little bastard tiptoes up behind you, taps you on the shoulder, and lodges in your head. Heinous houseguest. Night-wanderer. Attuner to the sounds of darkness.

IN NOVEMBER 2012, Dad was almost hit by a car as he crossed the street on the lam from his in-home nurse. Another day, he sat *working things out*, couldn't move, shackled to the confusion. His fingers played with invisible bits and bobs—weaving the air or grabbing at invisible bugs on the floor. These facts can be written, but they don't spell the man he once was—the guy I watched basketball with, who made me bananas and saltines fried in butter in a cast iron pan, who helped me build a tank system for a school project measuring oyster filtration, who rubbed my stubble and smiled when I came home with a shaved head.

WHEN THE FORGETTING was born, in the mix of disorienting diagnoses, an X-ray to Dad's abdomen uncovered a small hunk of a metal in his stomach. We marveled at its appearance, tried to explain the forgetting as heavy metal toxicity—a possible reversal on the horizon—but the inversion of reversal is stasis. No doctor bought our story. Like so many narratives, this one was left unfinished, its leaps unfounded.

I remember a story about him as a small child collecting blue gravel from the family driveway into a small chewing gum tin. He popped the round rocks into his mouth, eating them one by one. We reasoned in our desperation that a small piece of shale might have lodged in him forever—the way the poet Charles Wright, in *The Geography of Home*, remembers his time in California as "two yards and the flat back of the ocean, another tri-color splinter forever broken off in my heart."

LEVIATHAN OCTOPUS—a suction-cupped arm reaches out of the abyss. Sweet hereafter, let it be that heaven is a geometry. What does it look like on the other side of dementia when, neuron by neuron, in that silent apoptosis housed inside the skull, there's nothing left but tangles of dead pathways and fistfuls of plaque? Alzheimer's puts you in an empty room where keys get misplaced, lists get made and lost and rewritten and lost again— and as neurons die and roadways are abandoned in a five-finger spread through the brain's cortex, the vacancy reaches deeper and deeper into you until you don't remember new information, and the stories of your childhood are specters speaking to you out of the corners of rooms, or in your head, and then not at all. Then, everything's silent:

BEHIND HIS GLACIER-BLUE eyes was a landing strip where memories and reasoning touched down and alighted again with the aid of a majorly fritzed circuit board. Landmarks of navigation became apparitions entering and exiting the field depending on barometric pressure, energy flow, and electrical pulse. The self splits and mirrors the botched interconnections of a neuron forest or a madhouse cell division, and upon us is a whole generation of forgetters living in an age of left behind. Circles become two eyes inside a head: ghostly woman, her features always obscured by squiggles and scribbles. Out of atrophy's madness:

WHEN WE EXPERIENCE a work of art for the first time, what are we really seeing if not our own shadows? Our knowledge of the visual field is built around our experience of the world adjacent to our bodies. The *how does this make me feel?* moment, and momentarily I was devastated that my father had Alzheimer's, or momentarily I was ecstatic that he was making art. Of her encounter with a painting in a gallery window in Amsterdam, a painting that stopped her in her tracks, Jeanette Winterson writes in her essay "Art Objects," "Here was a figure without a context, in its own context, a haunted woman in blue robes pulling a huge moon face through a subterranean waterway." Winterson recalls that after her fleetingly intense encounter with this painting, she fled to the comfort of a bookstore where there were things she understood better than paintings, and how that moment compelled her to find a way of looking that garnered in her a true appreciation for painting. The same was true when I first encountered Dad's artwork. What to make of it? I had to find a way of looking, a context from which to view something wholly foreign. As Winterson writes, sometimes a work of art lives outside our initial ability to fathom it—out of fear or confusion or lack of practice. I began to understand Dad's artwork as a mirror of his confusion as well as his own desire to make sense of it.

As Dad and I painted together one lazy Wednesday, I chatted about a trip I took to England during which Parliament announced plans to rename Big Ben as Elizabeth Tower for the queen's Diamond Jubilee. "Kids go on that thing at school," he said, "and they throw 'em in there." He made a throwing motion, mimicking a child throwing an old toy into a corner, "Where is that thing? I don't need it." That day, I painted strange faces with horns, fangs, and bulbous noses. Dad painted dots and splotches, Pollock meets Monet meets Basquiat:

ART THERAPISTS, IT turns out, describe how art can calm Alzheimer's patients, help them express their feelings when words no longer do the trick. Occasionally, our painting sessions and their CD soundtrack initiate language: "This reminds me of my pot-smoking days," Dad said of the voices on a sixties greatest hits compilation. He'd tell me mixed-up family histories or mumble to invisible friends on the other side of the room.

The circular woman visited regularly during that time: a pumpkin head situated in a neat patch of Xs and Os, Os cascading from her skull, Xs marking age spots. Her eyes have been erased and redrawn, an eerie doubling effect. Her mouth is an open wound, bean shaped, and may have its own neck. Two circles where her ears might be. She's underwater or under cloud hair, or the haze of Dad's mind, and then she emerges whole:

"Turn it the other way. It looks like a house," he said. Rolls and reams of plans from my childhood. To be like him, I kept a notebook full of house plans, unmeasured but drawn and straight-edged in careful pencil. This is where the toilet is. This is the master bedroom. Neat capital letters, mimicking my dad's all-caps. Sometimes I'd add a round room for flair, and he never said, *No, that can't be done.* Dad hand built rooms in the houses we lived in tailored to our specific desires. I once had a whole up-stairs floor to myself. Bedroom, bathroom, walk-in closet. My brother Ryan got a loft with a ladder leading up to it where he kept his top-secret LEGO collection and a whole wall plastered with a map of the world. In those father-built houses, we were made to feel special. Dad was someone who could build you a house, and this shaped us. When the foundation of our meta-phorical house crumbled, we quite literally had a life's worth of physical corollaries from which to draw a comparison.

In his drawing of a house toppled over—part Modernist beast, part spaceship—floors connect at strange angles made for slip-ping and sliding so that every day's a game of downswing. Stairways lead into geometric attics with porthole windows. A square of grass on the ground floor—he's made us an atrium! Along the side of the house runs a lap pool, so he understands that water is a god, always the fish, never the bear. All the light is yellow in the rooms of the toppled house, the light of com-fort and birth. A disembodied face floats in a triangular room in the belly of the house. The face wears a perfect frown just below a blacked-out moon. The house is a galaxy. Straight black lines shoot out of the toppled house, overreaching perfection. Remnants of the underlying structure of a dying beast.

All houses protect, contain, decay.

Winterson explains the experience of really seeing a work of art as being dropped into a foreign city where "out of desire and despair, a few key words, then a little syntax make a clearing in the silence." In Dad's artwork there are clues and remnants flickering in cheap acrylic and marker. A small patch of light in the dark, an empty field akin to promise. Winterson asks, does art spark memories or does it create memory? If art and imagination go hand in hand, which of course they do, then the memories I created as a child, the ones I know are unreal dreamscapes but that I remember nonetheless as discrete events, do they become in retrospect art or memory? Likewise, what does Dad's art say about the space between his ears as he worked with fragments of ghost-memory like forgotten swimming pools in which time loses linearity and practices every stroke at once?

THE WOMAN AGAIN, finally in color and fully rendered, her hair a nun's habit. A nun from Catholic school? Dr. Frankenstein's Mona Lisa? One eye self-satisfied, a slit, the other eye a frightened doll's. Is she pieces of many women? The head to my headless nightmares? She's wearing glasses. The hint of a smirk in her magic-marker smile. Is that a mustache or is it teeth? The pieces don't fit, but they make a ghostly face. Her face is drawn in thick, black marker, but look at the shading beneath her left eye! Yellow and orange below, a light etched blue above. The intimations of a black eye. And her body a semblance. Childlike scribbles and jags. This could be a three-year-old's masterwork or a dark assemblage. Instead it's a rendering of regression. A thought bubbles against the woman's head. It's the same colors and scribbles as her body: greens, yellows, oranges, light-handed, tentative. A phantom appendage? A memory-in-flight? The eyes inside the thought bubble could be the eyes of an owl or a pair of lost visions. Inside the thought, the woman's twin, the never-born one, the one who lives just outside her, always a step behind. It holds everything escaped.

In Dad's artwork is the flesh-and-bone depiction of the surface of the moon. Winterson writes, "I do know that the process of art is a series of jolts, or perhaps I mean volts, for art is an extraordinarily faithful transmitter," the way that neurotransmitters are released and diffused across synapses, transferring impulse to fibers across the brain.

The language we use for artistic inspiration and for recovering memories is similar: sparks, flashes, jolts, volts, transmissions. Memory loss and creativity loss also carry similar language cues: dryness, emptiness, barrenness, block. You can't have one without the other. I know there is a shadow of my dad's former self precisely because he's painting, recalling events, and I'll know it's all dried up when his canvas remains empty as he stares and stares across the white space.

WHEN HE SAID to me out of the blue, "They have those round things," and his finger circled and circled the air, "from before I came here." Was he talking about clocks? Pac-men? When time existed only *before* Alzheimer's. Or when he asked my mom if she'd ever had children or "Do you live around here?" as they circled the neighborhood they'd lived in for almost eighteen years, maybe he didn't mean those things at all. Maybe he was asking her to pass the salt, to hold his hand, to tell him a story.

A chicken-or-egg scenario: There are two proteins gone haywire in the Alzheimer's brain: beta amyloids and tau, but who knows whether they are a cause or an effect of the disease. Or which is a cause, which an effect. All I know is that brain tissue dies as a result of their existence. Beta amyloid clumps, or plaques, build up between neurons and block communication between these nerve cells at synapses. If you look at illustrations of a plaque-infested neuron forest, you see nerve cells in the shape of oak trees, their root systems hung with balls of what looks like Spanish moss. Simultaneously, tangles form within cells. Where in healthy cells, the tau protein helps to keep food transport systems in straight, orderly tracks, in tangled cells the tau collapses and twists in on itself, the tracks fall apart, nutrients can't shuttle about, and the cell dies.

At a conference, an expert explained how researchers tested drugs for the "Swedish mutation," a genetic variation that guarantees early-onset Alzheimer's in about one percent of the Alzheimer's population, in which a series of misspelled DNA cause a variant in the amyloid protein. Once Swedish scientists found the mutation, they could test new drugs on mice bred with the disease.

In one experiment, two mice are placed into two separate water tanks, one healthy mouse and one Swedish mutation mouse, and are made to swim around looking for a submerged platform. The healthy mouse always finds steady ground. The mutated mouse, because it's already suffering from Alzheimer's, might never find the platform, just swims and swims and swims. These mice would drown if not intercepted. When researchers then inject the mutated mice with various experimental drugs, many of those mice find the platform, too. There are potential cures that cost billions of dollars to test on humans.

In one study, Dad was injected with a drug called Enbrel once every six weeks, with periodic spinal taps to ensure the Enbrel wasn't killing him in some other, horrible way. While we don't know whether he was actually on the drug during the study, we do know that when he received the drug after the study had concluded, because everyone who participates gets a chance after the fact, nothing changed, nothing we could witness, at least.

Dad didn't have the Swedish mutation, even though his father also had Alzheimer's, but he did have two genes called the APOE e4 gene, one from each of his parents. APOE genes range in numbers 1–4, and we all have them. Those people who carry the 4-gene from both parents have at least a tenfold greater risk of developing Alzheimer's. This genetic combination is not a guarantee, but it ups your chances.

Then the new theory: did football concussions catalyze the whole sequence of events? Dad was an all-state football player in high school and briefly played in college. When he had stories left to tell, we heard about how he got tackled, sewn up at half time, shoved back in for the second half, and subsequently blacked out and woke up in the locker room shower. He said after one of our painting sessions, "No more football for me. I stepped back. I said, *no more*. I got banged in the head three times." There's no one left who can tell us how many times he'd actually been concussed on that football field.

When he was fifty-two, Dad began to sleep more and more and all the time, his body preparing for what his brain had yet to discover. Mom began to feel lonely after dinner as he slept uncharacteristically in front of the TV. They'd built a marriage around doing things together—tearing down walls on a whim, painting rooms, digging holes—it didn't matter what. They'd loved work and doing work together, and they'd been talking about retirement as a time when they could play together as thoroughly and definitively as they'd worked side by side for thirty years. Mom threatened divorce to wake him up, literally open his eyes, get him out of his chair, but Dad's brain had already begun the factory production of the thing that would eventually kill him. He couldn't make himself stay awake; his brain was shutting down.

IN THE LANGUAGE of science, the physical locus of early Alzheimer's disease is the cerebrum: wrinkly and coiled like a packed jar of pickled pigs' feet. It's the stuff we see in our minds' eyes when we hear the word *brain*. The cerebrum makes up eighty percent of the brain's size. As the disease spreads throughout the cerebrum's lobes—frontal, parietal, temporal, and occipital—and the brain's cortex, where gray matter lives, you lose things like recognition, simple tasks, appropriate behavior, judgement, the ability to find the right words—Dad starts and stops stories twenty times a day—and, of course, memory. After you lose your short-term memory-making, the disease migrates to your long-term memories. The hippocampus, shaped like a seahorse, sorts and organizes memories into what we need to keep. When there are holes in your hippocampus where there used to be brain tissue, your memories lapse, fold in on themselves, loosen. Over time, the holes migrate, obliterating your everything-memory. You don't encode new information, and you relinquish all of the old stuff. Alzheimer's systematically destroys neurons so that there's no construction of the just-occurred.

A language we have yet to discover explains the world in plain, unfettered images. Its precursors—rather than alphabets and accent marks—are the viewfinder, the Venn diagram, the home movie, the black-and-white photograph. Then, the language of science with its apolipoproteins, receptors, amyloid precursor proteins, cutting enzymes called proteases that attack and cut the amyloid precursor proteins into fragments; phrases like cell death, memory loss, neurological dysfunction. Science is a language built on naming, but in the new language, the language we've yet to discover: the first time we played Pac-Man, the joy with which we vanquished all those little dots, floating fruits, and snarky ghosts by swallowing them whole. Or the snapshot of the first crab you ever caught with a halved mussel between clothespins, the brine and tin of its shell. The brain's multiverse where there are more planets than stars, more violent Big Bangs than leaves on trees that speak to each other through root and pollen, where silent reflection becomes the perfect communication.

FAINT WISP, THE lightest of all possible pencil marks, so delicate, but unmistakable as the same wraith vanishing into thin, electrified air. Woman in a brainstorm. Woman in locked synapse and frail-bone cage. *Let it come!* she's screaming. She is definitely screaming out of her slit mouth. When I asked Dad about this lady, a familiar wry smile crossed his face, a celebration of flesh, commemoration of a man in his decline, but he didn't have the words.

PHOTOGRAPH

Only that which narrates can make us understand.
—Sontag

AT THE HORIZON line, diagonals cross. Stars cross. Children cross streets without looking, as do men with demented brains.

We'd moved from Connecticut to South Carolina in a brown and tan Volkswagen Vanagon when I was five. About halfway through the journey, I became obsessed with speaking proper southern. I attached myself to the word *triangle*. Would a real southerner pronounce it *tri-angle* or the more elided, *trongle*? I practiced the two versions on my parents, who chuckled.

A child feels the displacement of a sixteen-hour move to a place where she knows exactly no one. A new, strict Catholic school— in another photo, I sit on a kitchen stool in my navy and white uniform, my head bowed, hands posed in prayer. The dog watches behind me—new apartment, everything new and glistening.

Were there darker, earlier pockets for my sadness? Mom's night visions, which became mine. Her cancer, which did not. Her anxiety, which did. Demons hiding in my closet. Migraine, the progenitor of sadness—or its manifestation. Another symptom of word-sickness: at seven, left alone with my grandfather while my parents went out, I cried and cried—secretly so Poppy wouldn't see—when I couldn't spell *acorn* correctly on my acorn-shaped homework page. It was a fireball in my sternum.

I frowned in school photos.

Migraines kept me locked away midday to dawn the next day.

I asked for bedtime poems about murder and death.

Age four, I asked my aunt to tie my hands and feet at the foot of the basement stairs so I could practice escaping up the stairs in case robbers came and tied me up.

A child holds danger just beneath her skin's surface. She holds and holds and holds until it blooms into something entirely other.

GHOSTS, MIGRAINES, AND VISIONS

I'm your unwilling wavelength.
                                        —Gail Mazur, "Dear Migraine"

The sea creeps to pillage,
She leaps on her prey;
A child of the village
Was murdered today.
                                        —Elinor Wylie, "Sea Lullaby"

AND TALKING IS everyone is everyone and talking is One
Loudspeaker Thing Christmas-dinner talking around the table
and the sound rises a sound-sun and belches and lets loose the
worst the most the drum-of-all-drums out of my head out of my
head out of my head out of my head and BOOM! and SPLAT! and
comic book thunder and comic book mallet and cracking bone
and it's bone and it's bone and it's bone that's done me in.

First migraine brought with it my first ghost. I was four. Cousin Kami and I wandered the halls of Gramma Bette and Poppy's house at Christmastime. I tasted dog food out of a bowl in the hallway. We ran around the place like dog cousins in our Underoos. We played Batman and Robin. I was always and forever Robin according to the laws of bigger, older cousins.

Holy Migraine, Batman. The world's spinning!

The lights glowed gold-holiday-Christmas, and they became brighter and brighter and brighter until I couldn't see. Aunts and uncles laughed all around me, which felt like a shark frenzy, a sickening collective cackle, the clanking of silverware, a storehouse of ignited emotion.

Gramma Bette placed a bowl of orzo soup in front of me at the dining table, and my vomit rose like steam over the bowl. I've never touched orzo again—you could say I'm haunted by orzo.

That Christmas Eve, my body became a channel through which intermittent pain colors the world around me. It was the first day of the rest of my life, and I heard, instead of the wise whisper of some long-dead migraine-laden ancestor, "Squawk! Caw! Ack! Gurrrble! Sting! Ack!" Because I was Robin. And here came the bad guy.

Holy bat-shark-lion-bear-rattler, Batman!

On my body's portage through the entrance hall of that first migraine, from the dining room to the white carpeted living room,

I looked up from Dad's arms to the second-floor landing where a woman stared down at me. Waist-length brown hair. Long-sleeve, floor-length white dress. In my memory she was named Sister Grace. *Did I really see her?* By then I'd started vomiting. Memories of a pink toilet bowl. A pain that only dark, quiet, and time would interrupt, but I didn't know it yet. First migraine etched itself into my newformed skull as the first time I saw a ghost.

Have you ever seen a ghost?
. . . It depends on what you mean
by seen.
　　　　　　　　—Cole Swensen, "Interview Series 1"

WHEN DAD WAS four, he loved to vacuum the house. One day as he was vacuuming the family couch, he saw a disembodied hand creeping up between the cushions.

Ghosts are everywhere.

The crow outside my window casts the ghost-caw of its ancestors. I hear footsteps at night. I walk down streets remembering who I was twenty years ago. Dad stumbles into my dreams, smiles, and behaves like he's in his right mind. To haunt is to show up somewhere regularly, ghost or human. To be haunted is to be present with a phenomenon that happens over and over again—an idea, a memory, a vision. Or to be haunted by something you can't get out of your mind. The memory of an event, a person, an old pair of shoes.

Migraines are just in the wrong place.
　　　—Andrew Levy, *A Brain Wider Than the Sky*

IF MIGRAINES ARE misplaced so is the person experiencing them.
I have always been in the wrong place: crisscrossing the country,
looking for something I can't name on the hazy embankment
of an imagined life. I have always displaced myself. When you
live at the edge of a place, at the edge of understanding, always
traversing borders both physical and emotional, you get to fab-
ricating pilgrimages. *Where am I?* is too easy, so you ask, *where
am I going?*

IN THE AIR, a conscious act of defamiliarizing, a dislodging of the birth relationship, and a reimagining of time. Residual ghost, I see Dad as a kid in still frames as if in a series of photographs. In one, he's sitting in the driveway of his parents' second-story duplex in Stamford, Connecticut. He's wearing suspenders and shorts, knee socks and sneakers. His light brown hair is neatly parted in an eternal school portrait. I see his sisters playing on the landing, one sister burning the hair off of another's Barbie dolls. I see Gramma Bette on the phone in the pantry hiding from the chaos, smoking a cigarette while talking to her own faraway sisters in South Carolina. I see my father collecting rocks. I see him vacuuming the green couch. I see him not as my dad but as his ghost. There are three childhoods: mine, and his, and his.

Maybe if I run down the street I'll catch up to myself.
                                                    —Dad

WHAT IT MUST be like to visit your childhood yard, stand in it, listen to the birds that used to sing outside your bedroom window,
and realize it's all a figment. That the yard of your childhood is
actually your mind, and little by little your mind's emptying of
its contents. And bit by bit you're becoming an empty lot.

WHEN I WAS a kid, demons hid in my closet. A man hid under my bed with a knife. Monsters tapped at my bedroom window. A woman wearing all white, tiptoeing on the rooftop, peeked into the skylights. My red carpet turned into a pool of blood when the lights went out. I was so haunted that I seldom made it through the night without relocating to my parents' bedroom floor. This happened until I was twelve. Even then, I was petrified to spend the night in my own room, but when finally I was banished, I lay on the cold brick floor outside my parents' locked bedroom door until dawn.

MIGRAINE HOUSES SADNESS and a game of wayward hide-and-seek where one self hides and the other seeks. Wayward things are difficult to control, unusual or perverse, the very definition of migraine. By nature, migraines belong in the loony bin. Look at the hours and hours spent jetting between dark bedroom and bathroom, pinball gone awry, then half sleep curled like a cat on the bathroom floor—one temple always cleaning the tile, then the shutdown into a penultimate sleep in which you wake up thinking you're better, emptied, and filleted. And migraine slowly crawls back into your periphery, starts over again, albeit briefly, and finally the ultimate sleep, from which you wake up weak, but alive.

TO REACH HOME is to be a redridinghood to reach there is a doll-house which is a Barbie house and train tracks upstairs and downstairs and so many shelves and pianos and cacti and in my bedroom the red carpet which is mine is blood which is the pumping sound in my brain and the fan klink klink klink klink klink klink but first is the kitchen

AT THE WORLDWIDE CHURCH OF GOD, our worship services were in a downtown storefront one year, a bingo hall the next, some years a Woodmen of the World insurance office—wherever there was cheap rent our congregation followed. The Church didn't believe in owning its own buildings because God's kingdom was coming. We'd soon be camped out in the Place of Safety, all of God's chosen people, while the Tribulation raged around us. I hoisted myself out of my metal folding chair, away from the two-hour sermon and fidgeting congregation, and into the winter parking lot. Migraine compelled me like a demon. If a voice asked, *remember all those shiny bits of shale twinkling in the sunshine?* I'd be the only girl nodding yes. Migraine suspended me between God and pavement. Between brick buildings, a parking lot packed with pickups, and a dirty, glass-hard inch of ice, I vomited on a short-stacked snow hill. Not much snow; enough ice to slip on. I wandered between cars in an onset daze. I slipped on the ice. Down hard, banged up, ass bruised, and my head full of tar black detritus.

In the backseat of the car where the sun tongued the window with such angled precision, I almost didn't mind the light all around even with nowhere to fix my head into, no pillow to hide in. But then I did mind it, or my head did. I slept through the service. I threw up all the hour's drive home, Dad stopping the car at intervals along the highway where I left puddles of bright yellow bile like paint splotched against green, green grass.

Like Dad's obsessive Xs and Os, preteen migraine forced acts of fixation. In my bed hovering over the sea of blood, I counted dryer cycles and ceiling fan rotations. Aroundandaroundan . . . Outside my room the world spun on, my brother constructing his LEGO cities or playing with plastic sharks, nauseating smell of dinner wafting under the door. Sometimes the sounds of a table saw. A hammered house project. But me, alone me, in bed me, counting. Whirthump. Whirthump. Fifty, sixty, one hundred rotations before the next wretch. The knobs on the pull chains knocked against each other. Three hundred, seven hundred six-ty-two, nine hundred seventy-five. Counting and counting and counting to forget. From a ceiling fan blade I could watch myself counting. Dislodged and spinning.

Or on the bathroom floor, two a.m., sweetest sweetest coldest tiles, big-toe frostbitten tiles. Ice queen dream tiles. In another dream, I'm a little girl in a red dress with a balloon in my right hand. I walk into a bathroom, but its size is wrong. It's fit for a giant. My bathroom and not mine, all cathedral ceilings, and a shower the size of a frozen waterfall, a cool and swimmable toilet bowl, porcelain of heaven, so white and inviting to sleep next to all night. Wrapped in a quilt, safe to throw up whenever I want, a bathroom fit for a queen's migraine dream.

I won't let myself be cut.

—Auguste D.

A REPEATING EVISCERATION. As a small child in Westbrook, Connecticut, in the summer, I pried open mussels to hang their guts from clothespins as crab bait. In South Carolina, later, Dad and I caught whiting and flounder from rickety piers or rock jetties. He taught me how to hook a bait shrimp, how to cast my rod, how to pull up a decent catch. I learned to descale and fillet. Once, filleting a whiting, we found millions of eggs as we fisted our hands into the guts. Below piers, through the fjords in deck slats, nurse sharks frenzied for chum—they could eat the shrimp off fishing lines with the finesse of a fine-fingered surgeon. Summers, we swam with those sharks in knee deep water, and Dad taught me to body surf beside them. Inherent danger in swimming with sharks. We must not take for granted the possibility of accident. Mythology smells like salt, seaweed, shark breath.

I COULDN'T PREDICT a migraine until I started yawning uncontrollably in the afternoon, a weird but unfailing precursor to my migraines that neurologist and writer Oliver Sacks calls a "characteristic feature" of the drowsiness that can precede migraine for many people. Then migraine was a punch card. I was a pretty nervous kid for various reasons including but not limited to wiring, and my nerves manifested in big, ugly headaches. They'd hit three-quarters of the way through the school day. I'd try to push until school got out but seldom made it without throwing up in the school bathrooms first. Once, in the sixth grade, all over the floor outside Mrs. Benson's English class. Home, my parents worried and helpless outside the shut bedroom door, all evening in bed except when I ran down the hall to puke. Repeat. Until about three a.m., at which time I'd fall asleep and wake up fine the next morning—a real girl again. Not a paper doll, not the rag doll hanging from a kite high in the air above craggy rocks, not a wraith or a potential victim of a supernatural murder. Not a wayward atom atop my own head. I was alive and strong and ecstatic.

MOM TAUGHT ME synonyms. Maps to making new meanings: *melancholy, ominous.* Mom tells me that when I was three, she passed my bedroom, watching as I stared wistfully off into space. When she asked what was wrong, I said, "I am melancholy, Mom."

"But why?" she asked.

"I just don't know, Mom," I answered with all my existential sadness circling the air around us.

By four, I'd found that rain clouds were ominous, full and dark. Synonyms were portentous of loss, my mind a cavern from which the future clawed. Synonyms for me became the doorway for making metaphor. Once, when Dr. Alzheimer asked Auguste D. her name, she offered him the month of May. Auguste was haunted by the revenants of words, or she was gifted a new language through which to see the world. When Dad witnessed a large woman and her gang stealing his belongings, he was showing me a vision of what life with Alzheimer's felt like to him.

SILLY WITCH OLD wives tale who boils boils toils and troubles cauldron of apple cider vinegar bubbles on the stove which is to say give it some power against migraine let it steam let it steam let it steam breathingbreathingbreathingbreathing brown towel-tented over the stove top imagine the migraine is a mushroom and you are its mother

CINDERELLA'S FORTRESS-MANSION looms behind a stone wall, pine trees obscuring its windows. I am next door to the mansion knocking at the back door of a neighbor's house, which is nothing at all like the fairy-tale house. This house is a one-story cement box painted peach. My mom has sent me there on an errand to borrow a cup of sugar. I knock at the door—I'm frightened already by the depth and darkness cast by Cinderella's house—even though it's sunny on the sidewalk where I'm standing.

The back door is ajar, but the screen door is latched. It's a bathroom door; the sink basin drips a trail of blood, but I stay where I am, small and petrified. A woman answers the door. I know she's a woman because of her pink velour jump suit, her breasts locked into the zippered top like the heads of two screaming children. Her bare feet are ugly and bunioned. I don't know she's a woman by her head, though, because her head's been lopped clean off. She's just a body, with a cleanly knifed neck, the meat of which looks like a marbled cut of raw steak. There is no blood draining from her, and when she speaks it's as if her head's been left on the toilet seat or on a part of the white countertop just out of view. She's telling me about an accident with a razor, but she's happy, chatty. The woman is outside with me now. She's shutting the door against the blood trail. We're both on the sidewalk, Cinderella's captive existence above us and surrounding us, and the woman is handing me a cup of sugar as I stare at her awful, gnarled toes.

104

MIGRAINES, ALZHEIMER'S, DREAMS, and visions are all anomalous, inconsistent with established patterns, or with established science, or acting at a variance, or out of the ordinary. Randomness has a lack of method, an irregularity like an arrhythmia. When something is random, it's weird, unusual, unexpected. A sudden outburst from a usually quiet person or a pair of invisible feet shuffling around on the dining room floor in the middle of the night. Anomaly fills a person with hope that anything can happen. The inner life extended outward like a hand is germane to experience. Your brain asks you to interpret the dream or the vision, and you listen based on your perspective. A lady who appears at the foot of the bed in the middle of the night—could be the Virgin Mary or the crackling memory of your grandmother. A dying man chatting with dead relatives. A slow dance with a giant God. Ghosts banished from frigid bedrooms. Living gnomes crouching in the bushes. A green hand creeping out of a living room couch. Strange lights and invisible friends. A warning in the voice of a shooting star. A vacuum-cleaner-in-the-sky, sucking cancer out of a body.

ON DECEMBER 23, 1862, in camp near Fredericksburg, Virginia, Confederate soldier (and my ancestor on Gramma Bette's side) David Ballenger wrote a letter to his wife, Nancy, describing something like the *aurora borealis* spread out in the sky over Fredericksburg the night after the second day of battle:

> there was a singular appearance in the elements, the most singular I ever saw in my life . . . It rose on the side of the Enemy, and came up very near parallel with our Line of Battle, and right over us. It turned as red as blood; but when it first commenced rising, it look more like the appearance of the Moon rising than anything else that I know to compare it to.

Shelby Foote in *Civil War: A Trilogy*: "to one Southerner it seemed 'that the heavens were hanging out banners and streamers and setting off fireworks in honor of our great victory'." Where Foote's anonymous soldier saw fireworks and honor, David saw *blood red* and *moonrise*. Interpretation of witness wrapped in nuance and personal symbol. David eventually hated war enough to want to defect (though he didn't), but not for the reasons I wish.

Haunted lineages.

THE WEEK BEFORE Christmas in 1996, a marking showed up on a glass building in Clearwater, Florida. The water stain was shaped like traditional statues and paintings of the Virgin Mary. Throngs of people made the pilgrimage to Clearwater, lit candles, and prayed for miracles in their lives. Believers saw a religious miracle; skeptics saw dried spray from a sprinkler system. What separates these witnesses? In *Thou Art That: Transforming Religious Metaphor,* Joseph Campbell writes, "And the deities that we once thought were out there, we now know, were projected out of our selves." One camp reflects its imaginative desires, "seeking to interpret the mysteries of the universe," onto the building while the other seeks scientific explanation. One camp wants to escape the confines of the flesh, the other revels in having its feet firmly planted.

In 1817, John Keats wrote to his brothers about the qualities he admires in a writer, what he called Negative Capability: "when man is capable of being in uncertainties, Mysteries, doubts, without any irritable reaching after fact and reason." But are we by nature content to simply let the world be? Are we capable of *not* seeking the definitive answers?

MIGRATE MIGRAINE TO the bathroom for the night blanket and pillow and coldcold tile set up a fort a fun fort it'd be once in not-migraine but in fun

LIKE THE CLEARWATER VIRGIN or the face of Jesus in a grilled cheese sandwich, objects/sights/experiences are imbued with meanings that fit into a cultural understanding of the world in which we either understand ghosts and visions as functions brain chemistry or harbingers of illness, danger, or even the supernatural. Maybe all three if we're lucky. Near the end of my mother's yearlong ordeal with a goat-demon-vision at the foot of her bed—I was four at the time and shared a bed with her some nights when my dad was at the nightclub they owned—she was diagnosed with a malignant facial melanoma. Harbinger, God, manifestation, or the unbelievable power of the human subconscious to know things before our conscious minds grab hold and interpret them, visually, as danger? I also saw a vision on those nights: a man in a white suit, smiling, who burst into flames but didn't burn, though she never mentioned her vision until I was grown.

MOM SAYS SHE was healed of the melanoma at a revival where she'd gone with my aunt to seek healing for my cousin Kris, who was born with a rare disease. She heard the sky open up, and it sounded like a vacuum cleaner, and it sucked all the cancer out of her. The experience becomes the self becomes the place of the self's annihilation. In two halves ever separated by a corpus callosum, tough body keeping self and self separate, a bundle of nerves that embodies division: left cells and right cells sequestered to indefinite solitude. If they could speak to each other, what would they say? There are people who think the next stage of human evolution exists in the reunion of the two hemispheres. For now, experience may sever itself from tangible reality. May be a ghost.

TAKE THE PILL with most ingredients the red one and go straight to bed but you can feel the over-the-counter under your counter and it makes you constrict your body and sweat bullets and in short far short it does nothing but constrict your vessels and make you smell your own blood

wake up wake up wake up wake up wake up wake up wake up like alarms clock alarms fire ones police ones

Cold pack heating pad dim lights caffeine meditation massage ginger magnesium feverfew butterbur peppermint willow valerian coriander seed Advil Aleve Motrin Excedrin Migraine triptans: sumatriptan (Imitrex Tosymra) and rizatriptan (Maxalt) dihydroergotamines Lasmiditan (Reyvow) narcotic opioid medications especially those that contain codeine chlorpromazine metoclopramide (Reglan) or prochlorperazine (Compro) beta blockers like propranolol (Inderal, InnoPran XL, others) and metoprolol tartrate (Lopressor). Calcium channel blockers such as verapamil (Calan, Verelan, others) antidepressants anti-seizure drugs like valproate (Depacon) and topiramate (Topamax) Botox injections calcitonin gene-related peptide (CGRP) monoclonal antibodies erenumab-aooe (Aimovig) fremanezumab-vfrm (Ajovy) and galcanezumab-gnlm (Emgality) sleeping and eating routines headache diary fluids exercise biofeedback riboflavin coenzyme Q10 acupuncture rosemary // Cholinesterase inhibitors: donepezil (Aricept), galantamine (Razadyne) and rivastigmine (Exelon) memantine (Namenda) safe and supportive environment omega-3 fatty acids ginkgo curcumin vitamin E exercise coconut oil coral calcium filtered water high-calorie smoothies music dancing reading gardening crafts acupuncture aromatherapy light therapy kami-untan-to huperzine A phosphatidylserine tramiprosate Mediterranean diet cannabis vitamin D3 sleeping position zinc avoiding aluminum astaxanthin rosemary oil frankincense oil

DURING THE TIME of my divorce and Dad's dying, each migraine threw out a new symptom, something just a little off, something I couldn't quite put my finger on. There might be a new pain behind my left eye in addition to my tried-and-true right eye. Or I'd throw up for two days versus the one day I was used to and end up in the ER, dehydrated and dumb. Or I'd wake up in the morning with a migraine emanating from my neck.

This one began after Massaman curry at the neighbors' house with sudden, uncontrollable yawning and vague anxiety—normal enough. I excused myself and walked across the lit yard, feeling the old hat: inexplicable anger and self-loathing. Then came some new symptoms: insomnia and a brainpan on fire until three in the morning.

A brainpan on fire, by the way, feels totally different than the normal ice pick to the back of the right eye. If this is a subtle delineation to a nonmigraineur, it is panic-inducing for me. I inexplicably and suddenly became a child trapped inside a burning house banging on paint-stuck windows. As I tried to read in bed—why?—migraine's fire blazed down my spine, into my shoulders where ice packs and iced drinks couldn't touch the flame. I panicked my way into fantasies about infection, curry fever, about the antidepressants I'd begun and ceased in a three-day span that week. I googled Serotonin Syndrome and twitching, wild limbs. Migraine turns you into a hypochondriac of the worst kind. The truth is, it was just another migraine, and migraine comes and goes for a grab bag of reasons.

At around two in the morning, I threw up. As I have my whole life, I vomited every half hour until ten the next morning, sleeping only in fits until the fist gripped my stomach again. There came a sleep reprieve until two in the afternoon, and I threw up again until eight that night. There are always a few hours in which the vomiting comes at an alarming rate, every five minutes or so, and I'm always on the verge of going to the ER—until I pass out that final time and wake up wanting something to drink, a sign that the nausea has passed.

After this migraine, I dreamed I was walking with the devil, who wore a top hat, on a high wire above sprawling red clay canyons. I was given a choice: stay with the shadow or fall to my death. The choice doesn't even make sense, but I stayed, kept my eyes averted, orbiting my own body like Tinker Bell. The devil said to me, *I'd like to see your permit for being.*

Because I need to memorize her expression is what I said about Auguste D.'s photo, and this could be true of all faces that mark time. If our synapses are fashioned by experience, forming our unique memories and selfhoods as they take shape; if we are us, according to scientist Joseph LeDoux, because of our unique synaptic cartography, migraine made me a fried, fireballed synaptic freak. In the ever-so-smallest way, migraine forced me to imagine Dad's brain-guilt when he said, *This is all my fault,* with his whole body. Like him, I blamed the misfire in my brain on my own neuroses—I'm too stressed, I eat the wrong food combinations, I'm bottling up my rage which dissociates as pain. Cluster. Synapse. Tangle. Plaque. In memoriam. Fire fire fire fire. Nerve endings: shot. Memory: it's almost boring how much we write about memory, refabricating memory. Sewing memory into fine strands of pseudo-coherence.

You look like a photograph of yourself taken from far,
far away.

        —Ani DiFranco,"Untouchable Face"

THE PLACE WAS crowded, close-quartered, rows of anxious writers and professors and students shimmying to the bar, booths and chair backs swamped with wet coats. Irish music and sporting events shifting through speakers. I'd been forgetting words, and my eyelids felt wet like an acid trip. Almost simultaneous with the waitress setting down a slab of meat, I toppled in the booth, curling up on some coats. My poet friends patted my head and asked, "Are you okay? Are you okay?" in that urgent kind of friend way. Their faces blurred.

"Yes, yes. No. I'll just go back to my room."

The pillows were perfect, so perfect that as the pain cut a fjord through my head, I was working out how to get one into my suitcase. I thought about the mania of the last few days and understood its roots. This was a clean-cut migraine from the crown of my head to the bottoms of my feet, the places yogis say we are rooted to the universe—the sky and the earth and our bodies in a vertical line.

In a gamble with migraine, I called home, almost immediately throwing the phone down to run to the bathroom. In my red and white polka dot pajamas, I threw up my guts all night, my body shaped like an upside-down L above the toilet or curved into a comma on the bed, underneath those perfect pillows. At about three a.m. I jolted upright, certain I'd been hit by shrapnel from a nearby gunfight, and then remembered where I was. Rick, my eternal friend and conference roomie, was asleep in the bed next to mine, but it seemed as though his head was miles away, untouchable, or head-shrunk. I felt, as I have so many times, like a paper doll version of myself.

Andrew Levy writes, "In my thirties, they were headbangers, once a month, like tiny anniversaries, rare enough to almost justify the feeling of clarity they brought afterward in the late afternoons." At thirty-four, I had little patience left for them. Gail Mazur: "whatever you were to me I've outgrown, / I don't need you, but you're tenacity embodied," and I thought, *yes, I don't need you*, and then I thought, *these pillows really are amazing.*

MARATHON GLAZED-BRICK HALL that is the corridor to another world—we know it is. In dreams, I need not use airline puke bag trash can brown highway shoulder grass middle school hallway carpet—anywhere Tupperware pasta pot plastic grocery bag vehicle air conditioning vent (projectile) but in real life I will use anything that catches.

WHEN I WOKE the day after the particularly ugly migraine to a world cleansed and glistening, what Sacks describes as "ensuing serenity and clear skies," I made some coffee. I read a book. I walked the dog, who sidled up to every wet branch and drank from every puddle like a proper dog. The sun was already hot, May in Florida, humidity only briefly swept aside by a post-storm breeze. Mangoes idled, heavy on their branches and almost ready for picking. The gardenias outside my office were just beginning to sour and fall, and above the old dog's grave mockingbirds and crows fought for territory. New boyfriend slept in the bedroom on a new bed.

It had been one those neck-graines, for which there's a story. I'd seen a chiropractor for shoulder pain totally unrelated to migraine. He was a stale-smelling, rotund, bald man inhabiting a bare-walled, broke-down office. He would wave little jars of strange substances around my body and test for weaknesses. After he had worked on me a few times with his ball hammer drills, I woke with a bulge in my neck one morning, and the migraine soon followed.

That particular morning, I called the chiropractor, told him he had to fix what he started. He agreed to meet me at his office on a Sunday. "I think your adjustments gave me a migraine," I said on his treatment table, hunched over so I wouldn't vomit. But I vomited in the office bathroom anyway.

"You're probably right," he said when I emerged, "you are such a good sufferer."

Fuck suffering.

The walk along the bay is serene, if baffling—no waves, clear water—as if the bay itself sees "a sort of walking miracle," like Plath's Lady Lazarus: reanimation as equal parts relief and inexplicable shame. The resolution of migraine is an emergence. I stare down at my feet glowing along the edges of stadium rows, at concerts, readings, and sporting events I've botched or missed. I walk along the outline of sky domes where the beach meets the horizon in a series of first kisses.

IN MY TWENTIES in Los Angeles, my neighbor gave birth to twins. I spent days with them watching the infants laugh at the ceiling of their 1930s bungalow, witnessing the discovery of *other* in each other's moon faces. Time was suspended when I was with the twins. We existed in a quiet, warm womb that was not really mine but that felt natural nonetheless, and I began to see myself as a twin in my imagination. In the dark at four in the morning, one breezy LA night when all the windows opened to the crashing Pacific, the rats skittered, and the night sounds of everything were amplified, I woke with a race-car heart and saw myself at the opposite end of the room looking at myself, a panorama of selves and selfhoods fanning like playing cards in a life-size deck. Light poured out of both our bodies. This was the first time I thought, *You look like a cutout of yourself across the room.* I was two people in a glowing blue room. I don't know why I experienced this dissociative twinning—something far away I couldn't yet deal with? My guardian self? An omen? A migraine aura? A unconscious fear of death?

During Alzheimer's, there were two of Dad. His real self and another guy. In the beginning, Dad would call this other Al Heimer, and Mr. Heimer was definitely another person: unfunny, confused, out of his mind, clumsy, batshit crazy. My parents developed a shorthand concerning Al. Mom would ask, "What's my name?"

Not knowing the answer, Dad would say, "Al's here." Or wondering why the coffee mugs are in the oven, she'd ask *why*.

"It was that other guy," he'd say.

In between she spoke repeatedly of "twins."
—Dr. Alzheimer on Auguste D.

They say meeting your doppelganger is a forewarning of your imminent death.

Percy Bysshe Shelley saw his doppelganger before he drowned. Mary Shelley wrote in a letter to Maria Gisborne an account of her husband's experience, ". . . he told me that he had had many visions lately—he had seen the figure of himself which met him as he walked on the terrace and said to him—'How long do you mean to be content?'"

He died soon after.

In his autobiography, *Truth and Poetry: From My Own Life*, Goethe saw his doppelgänger—double-goer—riding past him on a horse on the way to Drusenheim. The twin wore an unfamiliar gray suit with gold trim. When Goethe rode the route again years later, he looked down and realized the suit he was wearing matched his doppelgänger's those years before. He was strangely reassured by his vision, as though through his twin he'd stumbled upon the evidence that he did, in fact, exist in the world.

Dad became his own liminal space, the tightrope between his former self and Al. His doppelgänger reassured him.

WITH A SECOND self, the possibility of leaving the world completely can be less like a cliffside and more like a shoreline. The opposite of splitting is becoming. The opposite of becoming is forgetting. There is the self who embraces death and the self who runs. What better place than in the brain to proliferate these entanglements: cell-world, atom-world, zero-point energy of innerness?

As Levy tells it, Carl Linnaeus, the famous botanist known for creating our modern system of taxonomy, binomial nomenclature, saw himself outside himself, too, in the midst of a migraine aura. Once, when he opened a door to another room: "Oh, I'm there already." To be in two places at once, to loose the shackles of learned physics, is an act of the mythmaking mind. I've felt it happening during a migraine—some inkling of a double life, a symptom of migraine's aura but also a symptom of a conjuring mind. From his *Book of Imaginary Beings*, Jorge Luis Borges: "Suggested or inspired by mirrors, the surface of still water, and twins, the concept of the Double is common to many lands." Mirrors. Still waters. Myth warns us that we all die of the beauty of our own reflections, shackled to them like Narcissus. A twin reflection reminds us that we're alive.

IN THE MIDST of a deranged mess in Dad's wardrobe—an antique gun, a woven leather police beat stick, wadded-up toilet paper, coins, pencil nubs, adult diapers, cuff links from the old church days, notes, and drawings—scrawled on crumpled yellow legal pad pages, I found the story of how my parents met:

The year was 1973. When our story was born, it was a beautiful fall day. In New England . . . and school had just started. A new place, a new time . . . hoping to make new friends and start anew.

He'd left football in Tennessee to return to Connecticut and a new college.

Standing in the hall at the gym. Just scoping everything out. I remember thinking, "She's not bad. Look at her, she's not my taste . . . there are too many to see. Maybe I'll leave." Right then at the front door I see this girl riding her bike into the gym. I've got to meet her! She must be crazy. No one rides their bike on the gym floor. All jocks know that. I asked her what she was doing . . . She replied, "this is a new bike, and I have nowhere to lock it up." I said OK and fell in love at that moment. I didn't let her out of my sight.

Which was basically true for thirty-five years.

Almost forgot to get her name, Rita. And she's Italian. I left walking on air. At that moment, I fell in love. When will I see her again? Will she want to go out? I'll see.

. . .

Sandy and Rita went to the Halloween Party, and so did I. There were 100 people in a two-bedroom apartment. The floor started to give away. I was keeping a close eye on Sandy and Rita . . . I got them out of there. So after that bad party, Rita and I started seeing each other almost daily, that made me very happy.

The first trip to Stamford, my hometown, Rita came on the train to meet my family. As the train pulled into the station Rita was standing at the train door as it came to a stop. Seeing her, I fell in love even more than I did the first day at the gym a couple of months prior.

Her smile made my heart almost stop. Her kiss was as sweet as a kiss could be.
34 years have passed, and I love you more today than ever. Thanks my love. Bo.

The last love letter he'd ever write.

In a twinning that takes a creative act to perform, Dad saw quite viscerally the two sides to his condition, a dissociation from his former self and a simultaneous act of metaphor making:

I read the story aloud to him one day when he couldn't read anymore, and he said, "Man, he sure knows more about me than I do."

WHEN THE WOMAN and her gang arrived every night at ten o'clock to make Dad dance and to mess up his belongings, he told me, "Well, our friends came in, and they ruined everything. They said it was all wrong so they tore it all up and made things dirty again. I told them to give me thirty seconds, and I'd leave, but they didn't care." From real events sprung gangs of bullies to explain everything from his newly made mess to his incarceration and "those people" who wouldn't release him to walk down the street—vestiges of a metaphysical longing for order we all seem to share. And were these the same friends he joked with when he thought no one was looking? Were they manifestations of the intruders in this head, the blown-up cell transport systems and sticky drapery blocking communication? Were these memories rogue imaginative leaps?

I SAW DAD'S ass caked and crusted with old shit because he forgot how to wipe himself. Proof of reality being askew. No myriad interpretations here. Shit stains all over the place—his underwear, the bed he shared with Mom, a light switch. I witnessed this unwillingly. To penetrate language, to find its truth in the offal, its echo between earth and sky, I must describe an ugly phenomenon and let it haunt me.

EXPUNGE YOUR GUTS until you're spitting bile and bile and yellow mustard yellow bile scientifically interesting both practically horror show

From Elizabeth Bishop's "The Fish": "I caught a tremendous fish / and held him beside the boat / half out of water, with my hook / fast in the corner of his mouth." The poem's speaker contemplates her fish for a long time: his skin that hangs in wallpaper strips, his flesh packed like feathers, his isinglass eyes. Metaphor is truer than the fish itself, and its weight—the power of language to describe the thing—becomes inconsequential as the poem's speaker succumbs to experience so that after all of her meticulous capturing and recording, the last line of the poem reads, "And I let the fish go." How do you let it go? If you want to keep it, how do you let it go? How to disembowel a threshold of blood? To let go is to embody the letting, to split open and let oneself fall to the floor.

A LAMPLIGHT IN Florida's mangroves, their fingerling roots and pneumatophores sucking air from my lungs.

My head's a popcorn machine brimming with stenciled stars: water from high-chlorine content floods my nostrils; or citrus fruits; or hyperactive neurotransmitters. I've been a swimmer even when I wasn't swimming, an explorer of the underbelly of beds and the bowels of closets. A sailor in the toilet bowl. The girl who *might have been* as much as the girl who *is*. Simultaneously the girl who looked back and the one who kept walking.

Ooze of chemical release, the factory-style increase in neurotransmitter productivity as serotonin, dopamine, and norepinephrine bubble out, as vessels expand to bursting. Warmth and sizzle and star map lightness all over—like falling headfirst into a bowl-shaped sky. There's no hitting the brain's pause button even if the show is too much to watch.

VISION OF A man in a white suit, who bursts into flames at the foot of the bed.

A friend named Goona-ghana—a dark blob, a more than shadow, Grimace in Hell—who followed me around like a benevolent spirit, a memory drawn and redrawn over the years.

Waking up to the smell of putrid flesh in the middle of the night.

Invisible paws traipsing over my body at night, disembodied purring.

Experiencing my own birth on LSD, the hot, pink suffocating fluidity of it.

Full-bodied apparitions wearing down jackets, footsteps in the hall, orbs bursting through windows when asked politely to leave, a door knocking loudly with no one behind it.

On mushrooms, a breathing earth, black birds in the bedroom, a door knocker with the face of a live, yawning woman.

Doing laundry, Dad's underwear full of shit. It's all a wild dream.

IN THE AIR around these stories, leftover molecules existing only in certain light.

AND HOW THE night's begun under a setting fettering body your tiny bird-bone body its tireless childness or the day it'll give up the ghost

PHOTOGRAPH

As photographs give people an imaginary possession of a
past that is unreal, they also help people to take possession
of space in which they are insecure.

—Sontag

IN THE WORLD of the apartment complex photograph, we lived two buildings away from the pool: apartment A201. We lived up a flight of narrow stairs in a two-story condo. In a storage closet at the top of the stairs, I kept caught ocean things: coquina clams, tiny fish, sand dollars in buckets of seawater until they died. I was afraid in this apartment, of my glow-in-the-dark rosary beads and Madonna figurine. I was afraid of the punk-rock babysitter's stories about a ghost-woman who walked our roof on rainy nights looking for her lost love. I was afraid of the space beneath my bed, of the cracked bathroom door, of the clock's ticktock, of shadow and shadow and shadow.

Can a photo portend a future? It would be Dad later who would carry me out of my parents' bedroom in the middle of the night, lock the bedroom door, pretend not to hear as I begged to be let back in.

THE SEPARATE LEAVES

Dr. Alzheimer: Are you sad?
Auguste D.: Oh always, mostly not; it happens that one sometimes has courage.

Dear Lion-dragon,

This is for your black ballooning head and your train-track red body. For your eighteen legs and the blue ocean roiling around your head. Your eyes are so sad! Blue-green radiating out of the war paint on your face. Brushstrokes like bullet holes into your heart, and part of your animal body is also a man's body. Red legs, red arms, red chin reaching into your melancholy. Is this the way you exist in the world now? Is this your vision of yourself, as disconnected parts, bodies morphing, and a head too big to hold?

They say you were ten pounds of head when you were born.

We stand at the edge of everything. We stand confronting moronic oblivion. In this particular dream, which is a dream of reality, I'm not jostled when you make word salad or when your eyes don't register *the thing itself* or when you paint hieroglyphs with the most tentative hand. You are here and everywhere, Dad. And tiny particles of you have escaped from your skeleton so that you're dancing in Rome and snorkeling in the Florida Keys and playing catch in New Mexico and flying figure eights between the Andes all at once. You're a small boy in knee socks, a hunky football player, a man in love, a builder of solid worlds, a kind soul. You're laughing at gibberish here with me. We're laughing together. We're escaping memory's sine curve. Just this once, we're flying out of orbit, we're watching the ropes unravel in the ripples and limbs of the sky.

. . . and if I find you I must go out deep into your far resolutions / and if I find you I must stay here with the separate leaves.

—A. R. Ammons, "Hymn"

WE LISTEN TO Christmas music. We sing along. The end is a final confluence that snakes out of time, into space, a river with a new name. If I was, and still am, haunted by Auguste D's eyes, the eyes of a woman long dead, is she yet alive? Senses, a Morse code, a radical light, as Ammons calls it in another poem, bouncing around in the skull. In the photo of Auguste D., I see in her eyes a cellular knowledge, an end and a beginning, as if she recognizes the camera trained on her as the face of her husband or as a teapot reminding her to boil water. You hear music all the time; I catch you sitting by yourself humming to the music of the spheres. *Musica universalis*: Alzheimer's lets you hear it, the dance of the Sun, moon, and planets.

WE'RE SPENDING A few days together while Mom is out of town. I've never stayed the night alone with you during Alzheimer's, and I decide to stay on the living room couch instead of in another bedroom in case you try to go for a midnight stroll. You've started wandering, and I'm afraid you'll wander away from me. A few weeks before this, Mom in the next room playing internet backgammon, you flew the coop. Mom recovered you out wandering the streets, sweaty and smelling of smoke.

You're an unexpected birth, eyes wide in the dark of midnight. I open my eyes in the blue-dark. Your hand reaching out to me, "You're still awake," you say, thinking I'm Mom. "Come to bed."

In the morning, your lip's sliced. I imagine you in the dark, feet dangling from the bed, thinking it's morning, or not thinking but acting. You'd felt your way to the bathroom in the dark. You picked up the razor and began to shave, night a playground, an open hunting season on rote activities, things familiar, things mentionable. Reality carrying less and less meaning. So I hide the razor in another drawer for another night. You also changed clothes all night, blooming piles of clean or dirty strewn around the room: sweatpants, underwear, socks, a button-down shirt, a windbreaker.

When I was small, I used to thumb through that huge, cloth-covered book of yours called *The Twentieth Century*. The mug-round coffee stain on its cover, its photos of naked, dead bodies contorted in pits outside of concentration camps. I was too young to understand what the bodies signified, who they were. I could read, but I couldn't understand. I could not process so much destruction as those bodies, legs and arms protruding, shaved heads at various impossible angles, but I couldn't look away either.

BECAUSE OF THIS fraught night, or out of this night, a migraine etches its shape onto my brain, just a tickle. Today we're visiting a new daycare.

At your last daycare, you managed to escape before we could get you, cursing a chasing volunteer as you ran down the road screaming *Fuck*. Kendal, home from college, found you on the roadside. You punched her car, pushed her, accused volunteer aide of hitting you.

The silence between us reverberates in the here and now; I am bursting out of the car's hull, Dad. You've driven me hundreds of hours in cars: to school in the morning, home early from school during a migraine, church sports tournaments, weekly church services, family vacations, east coast moves and visits back and forth from South Carolina to Connecticut. We'd driven together punctuated by silence and sixties music. I am a traitor as the gulf between us grows vast and unswimmable. Alzheimer's is like Andrew Levy's migraine: a zebra in the kitchen. We are in the wrong place driving to Adult Day Care. I drive you, age fifty-nine, to daycare.

We've closed a gate on something we can't recover from. Every time you say, "I'm turning a corner. I want to live," your hope morphs into delusion, the handwriting on the wall of your mental state. We sit in the car. We drive to the next room. A corridor in which you will find errant fingers in your spaghetti, in which you'll think you are being attacked in the front yard as you move the trashcan in circles. You say to me, "I can't live like this."

At the new daycare overlooking a canal and a tree-lined bike path, a man named Keith waves. "This is where they keep the rowdy ones!" he yells from a group of people sanding and painting blocks, drawers, and wooden flowers. You trail me warily as we visit the facility's rooms. A sewing circle, a large singing group. The craft group, which also doubles as a chill-out room, consists of a few skittish people who need low light and calm. On their table, a lantern radiates soothing colors in the shape of butterflies like an infant's nursery. A lovely woman with dancing eyes and shiny, long, white hair cuts pictures of kittens out of a magazine. "See these two?" she asks.

"See how they're squeezing each other? My mother has lots of cats," she says. She passes her kitten cutout around the group, making sure everyone handles the picture. You roll your eyes—we've always rolled our eyes at each other to signal a private joke.

Later, the daycare director asks you if you want to make an appointment for a morning visit. "I'll have to think about it," you say. I make the appointment anyway. And as we head out to my car you say, "I don't think I'm ready for this." A low buzz all around us: cicada song.

I explain that we need to be ready. Mom can't bring you with her to the kitchen showroom anymore, and the old facility can't seem to hold onto you. It occurs to me that I am incarcerating you, shoving you into a drawer. I want to grab you and hold onto you forever. That, or run far away. On the hot asphalt beneath branching southern oaks, I'm a kid again. For years, migraine had held for me what I couldn't hold myself—it cupped my anxiety, my shyness, my congenital sadness, my intractable night fears. I had swallowed all of it whole, and migraine had allowed me to release them in violent explosions. Without migraine, I might have melted away. I feel that old fear now, like a jagged rock in my pocket.

"This place isn't so bad," you nod.

It's here. It's everywhere. Father and daughter standing in the parking lot of the Senior Friendship Center, both of us too young for dementia but thrust into its arms nonetheless. The sun is so hot that sweat drips from the trees above us. Herons and egrets throat moan. Just-parked cars click and rattle as their air conditioners wind down. We are two wings standing in a cutout of space. Around our bodies, summer air thick enough to drink.

Back in the car, silence cellophanes us. Aberrations tickle my throat. Migraine blooms. Disease without answers becomes a fixed ghost. Horizons are terrifying if you're swimming out to them. I flip on Bruce Springsteen's "The Ghost of Tom Joad" to preoccupy us. You tap your fingers on your knees, bobbing your head. The Boss tells us to keep driving, keep rolling: "we're goin' someplace there's no goin' back."

At home, I prepare for the day's deepening migraine in a dark room, the massacre in Sandy Hook on the television in the living room, dead children invading my psyche, turning migraine into a terrific nightmare. Maria watches you, her son-in-law, the laws of the universe misaligned. I am in charge, but I can't take care of you. I can't move except to puke in the bathroom. My unexpected child, I can't keep you safe.

ON SATURDAY, YOU'RE having a tirade about the invisible people who won't let you walk down the street to buy cigarettes. *Them* again. "It's unconstitutional," you say, "my son, the governor, should know about this." You escalate, eyes widening. There is a grain of truth in your delirium: Ryan works in politics. Mom won't let you outside alone. You yell with eyes blearing and begging, wide blue tunnels, gut frenzy in your green leather recliner.

You tell me for the fifth or sixth time that the cat's about to die. I can't look at you, Dad, your sporadically shaved face, a few cuts here and there, your eyeglasses gone—lost in the ocean the day we all tried to play at the beach—your hands that won't sit still. That day at the beach, you tried to make out with me in a haze of late-stage antipsychotics.

I am post-migraine, spent. All I can think to ask is, "Are you hungry?"

"Yes," and that's that. We have lunch together, all agitation gone.

When Dr. Alzheimer asked Auguste D. to recite the alphabet, after a feeble attempt she replied, "Oh please, I'm not dressed for it." When you pee on the kitchen floor, you say, "Somebody put the bathroom in the kitchen." Alzheimer's has its own logic. The only thing left for you is eating what's put on your plate.

Later in the day, I usher you into the shower. Your naked body still well-built, your penis wagging. You have no modesty left, and I ignore my own. I hand you a bar of soap and remind you what to do with it. I pour shampoo into your hand and tell you where to put it. I don't care if you emerge clean, just that we get through this embarrassment. I wash a load of clothes: under-wear soiled with shit, wet socks.

Dr. Alzheimer asked Auguste D. her husband's name. She didn't know it, answered, "My husband isn't here right now."

We construct Mother's Day cards for the upcoming holiday. I learn how to be a nursery school teacher: spread out the art magazines, a pair of scissors, glue. Guide your hand. You look through each magazine for pictures you like. You choose paintings of houses surrounded by neat shrubs and picket fences. You choose a canvas full of brightly colored buttons. These are things of the home, domestic signifiers, things that remind you of a home you helped create, at the center of which is Mom. You can't cut anymore; instead, you shred and tear with the scissors.

You rip out a page featuring a painting of a sailboat and bluest ocean. We arrange all of our pictures in front of us on the table. "Making cards is a lot like planning a house, isn't it," I say, thinking blueprints and puzzles but really just chatting to fill the space. Instead of lightening the mood, I remind you about what you can't do.

"I guess it is," you say, and you cry as you glue images to paper with the gusto and imprecision of a first-timer. Our images are wavy and lumpy against the thick sketchbook paper we fold into cards. I write out Happy Mother's Day for you to copy, but in the "H" of Happy, you see two sticks and a lump.

"Would you like me to write it?" I ask.

"You'd better," you say, watching me form the letters. When we get to the inside of the card, I ask what you want to say. "Love forever, Bo," you say, crying again. Somewhere in that ball of frayed wires and collapsed telephone poles, you have reimagined the notion of forever. I wonder if you're already flying above me.

PHOTOGRAPH

*What photography supplies is not only a record of the past
but a new way of dealing with the present.*

—Sontag

WHAT INVISIBLE ROPE connects father and daughter? I did not come into being connected to this man by umbilical cord. I didn't eat his placental lunch for nine months, nor feel the underwater warmth of his womb. I didn't suck and chew on his breasts until they bled. I never told him in a fury that I hated him.

Dad told me episodic bedtime stories about a cast of characters called Little Eagle, Wise Turtle, and Old Man in the Mountain, endured my obsession with Duke Blue Devils basketball, drove me to church volleyball tournaments across the state, hours in the car together where we listened to Tommy James & the Shondells, singing along to "Crimson and Clover," in our un-tuned voices.

Dad smelled of sawdust and Listerine.

Dad went out for Sunday donuts.

Dad smoked in secret.

Dad was always in the room, even when he wasn't.

Beside me, holding me up, at the pool in an apartment complex in a new land.

Fathers and daughters speak in an unspoken language. I never needed to cut the rope that bound us, nor did he need to assert its existence.

YOU DON'T MIND

Anger is displaced in all directions and projected onto the environment at times almost at random.
—Elizabeth Kübler-Ross, *On Death and Dying*

IN ARID REGIONS a bilateral fear of forgetting requires no water to grow. A xeriscape. To move across country to watch your father's mind melt into a patch of dry land is to plant a desert garden. To remember that his own father's mind did the same. To understand that we, too, could have the right genetic cocktail, me and Ryan and Kendal. The two halves of our bodies, themselves squabbling siblings, join forces in this fear. We pad around our houses unsure of what to do next, the paralysis of forgetting grips us with winch hands. We loathe our sunbaked selves.

SOME DAYS IN Florida in the humidity and endless sun, I lived in an X-ray of *fucking pissed*, petrified in my bones. What if, one day, I were to ask my husband, "Have you ever been married?" The personality change of someone with Alzheimer's is plateaus hyphenated by sheer drops, drastic and unmitigated. One minute a man, stoic all of his life, will weep like a child. The next, that same man, gentle all his life, will grab his wife so hard by the wrist that she's bruised for a week. Before daycare, Dad's complaint became, "I have nobody to talk to," as though he knew that his new language was special to a new social order. But he also didn't want to hang out with elderly folks. He knew he wasn't one of them. I concluded that all was desert just as sure as Earth revolves around that big orange ball in space. Where does the confluence of past/present landscapes leave anyone? On an x-axis, we are the horizontal movement. When I played in the pool with Dad, throwing a spongy football back and forth or racing from one end to the other, if he imagined that he was eighteen again, was it so? Had he crossed over into negative x?

In *The Astonishing Hypothesis: The Scientific Search for the Soul*, Francis Crick, codiscoverer of the double-helix structure of DNA, calls humanity a pack of neurons. Like twinning and double-living, electrically excitable cells rend in half, too, in an X-acto process called cytokinesis. From the Greek, cell motion. Cell movement. If you can imagine the explosion of tiny particles bouncing around as indiscriminate little bumper cars all over your left arm, you can imagine a cleavage furrow forming, you can imagine one world become two.

I WATCHED MYSELF on late-night TV. Strange experience. Cytoplasm rends into two daughters. Me and you. I and we. They are two. Cytokinesis makes sure generations are copacetic, X chromosomes split and hasten their diatribes. In some organisms, a wall's erected in the splitting. You stay on your side. I'll stay on my side. We'll dwell in the same city space, separated by a chalky line drawn on the sidewalk. Sometimes when you're two people, the wall is translucent. The moon or a spotlight erected by one of your selves. "Hey," she'll call, "look at me over there."

Splitting of the cytoplasm. The very material within a breathing cell.

An act of breaking apart.

An act of taking and breaking.

In real life this doesn't always make two beautiful Xanadus. Sometimes it makes one awful, broken thing like a massacred wing or a xenografted hand.

THE MAN NEXT to me on the plane from Tampa to Los Angeles smelled like Jack Daniel's and high school locker room. He picked his nose, rolling his boogers into neat little wads then popping them into his mouth.

"My mom just died," Jack Daniel said, "Yeah, I'm in Tampa for the funeral. It was sudden, really sudden." He pointed to the *Rolling Stone* in my lap, a black-and-white photo of a young Hunter S. with a cigarette, smoke swirling around his hand and over his eyes. "Great man, great man," he said. Painted on Thompson's face was that old road map for dying: going out big. *Do not go gentle. Better to burn out than to fade away.*

Jack's mom probably died quietly in her beachside condo, but its abruptness jarred him into recollection: she was buried in a lightweight pine box, he told me, and during the funeral her box, with her inside, swayed back and forth in the slight Gulf breeze. Afterward his sister had said, "Gee, I thought she was going to get up and walk away."

Jack's sister tried on their dead mother's bras and underwear after the funeral. The older generation prepared to sit shiva in their black outfits, taping up the windows, while the younger generation of sons and daughters, cousins and nieces, went to a bar and got shit-faced all night long. He was still drunk at the terminal. He told me about his wife back in California keeping an eye on the engraving shop, even though she was a science teacher, and how they'd met during their three-year stint in the Israeli army but didn't see each other again for seven years—when he got a computer and looked her up online. How he really loved to stick it to the man, just like Hunter S. did.

He recounted the story of how back in Los Angeles he had to donate a hundred bucks to a city official's election campaign in order to get a stop sign erected on his street and how that had made him feel ashamed. How, weeks later, and just as he finished off a joint in the back of his engraving shop, a candidate for mayor waltzed in to solicit votes, how he'd stood up to the candidate saying, "I don't want a fucking brand new downtown, I want a mayor I don't need to bribe to get a stop sign put up on my street so the fucking kids don't get run over by your fucking renegade Porsche."

As we deplaned in LA, Jack said in a sort of afterthought "Hey, we're all shit. We fuck everything up. We don't care about anything." At baggage claim, he hugged his wife and cried.

IN HIS ESSAY "The Edge as Threshold," Gregory Orr writes, "A poet needs to go to that place where energy and intensity concentrate, that place just beyond which chaos and randomness reign." To thrive on thresholds is to love the possibility of crossing them or to feel the comfort of their presence as untraversable spaces. Depends on your temperament. Docks, shorelines, doorways, cliffs, bridges, lips, window ledges, hiking trails, stoplights, stop signs, welcome mats. Threshold as an act of collision. Centrifugal force. Time-stamp delegation. Two parts, or four, or five make something whole from the broken latitudes and borders of separation. And you are here, and I am there. We are far apart, dots on that old spectrum, but then someone, some part of the whole, gets sick, gets dying, and there it happens: a reassembly of the present tense in which stories are told, ancient solid beings of light and voice.

THRESHOLDS REMIND US of the solo journey. In 1818, German landscape painter Caspar David Friedrich composed *Wanderer in a Sea of Fog*, a painting in which a man in a black suit stands on a cliffside contemplating the continents of impenetrable fog below him. The man leans to the left, shaken off-kilter by the mystery of his view. This is Romanticism's emphasis on the individual, on the creative moment, the lone subjectivity of the self. In the end, whichever end is ours, we're doing it alone. We will see the people around us dying; we may even hold hands with their dying, but they alone walk through the door. The opposite of together is alone, is parting, is rending, dividing, leave-taking, separation. A line in the sand, drawn.

THRESHOLDS REMIND US of danger. In "Theory and Play of the *Duende*," Federico García Lorca explains that *duende*, that dark creative energy pulsing through the belly of the whole planet, "loves the edge, the wound, and draws close to places where forms fuse in a yearning beyond visible expression." Should we fall into the wound, would we be infected by something too dark to shake off? This is the question. Vision and memory collapse-collide-collude-coalesce into a screaming mass of electro-pop colors and sounds. I can hear the piano keys tinkling, the repeated arpeggios of everything I'll never remember and the nothing I'll always see. Experience is a room, and in the room archetypes float—little gods—like comic book thought bubbles, dismantled doll parts, cut pigtails, bodies of lint, fire, and moon. Vision and memory are bedmates, the convergence of high and low ground. All remembering is a lie, all vision is seen once and dies.

THRESHOLDS REMIND US of possibility. Orr writes that there can't be creative energy without the possibility of chaos. Inertia at the shoreline is the death of imagination. There are over eighty billion nerve cells in the human brain with branches connecting at trillions of points, each point a threshold unto itself. The possibility of connection has endless iterations. In apophenia, the experience of seeing patterns or connections in unrelated things, years of magical thinking result in magic. We find examples in literature: Nabokov's "Symbols and Signs," in which the story's unseen protagonist "imagines that everything happening around him is a veiled reference to his personality and existence," or Pynchon's *The Crying of Lot 49*, or Eco's *Foucault's Pendulum*. Does it matter that the characters engaging in imaginative acts of possible connection, in following the rabbit down the hole, might just be insane?

THRESHOLDS REMIND US that we live in a landscape of no answer, of here and everywhere, that questions—not answers—are the real stuff of living. Across that threshold, the application of a false if/then relationship. I heard this kind of logic a lot in Church: She had a baby who was disabled because she had an abortion when she was seventeen. He drowned in the river because he was out partying on the Sabbath. A secret relationship between reality and imagination forms in order to make sense of outcomes. Sometimes this line of thinking causes mass death and destruction. Other times it's just nice to have an imaginary friend under the pillow.

Can we experience the world outside ourselves with acknowledgment that our brains can also communicate between thresholds, between real and imagined? That the imagined life might feel as real as the corporeal one? In *The Poetics of Space*, Gaston Bachelard writes that memory plus imagination equals recollection. Straight memory, according to Bachelard, is just like showing houseguests around the rooms of a house for the first time: *this is the bathroom you'll use, this is the bed you'll sleep in.* Imagination is where the house comes to life with all of its aromas and sounds and emotional turning points.

CRESTING A HILL on I-10 headed into Los Angeles. Rush hour. The city below took my breath away, and this was not a good feeling. I had never seen so many cars under one sky, and everyone doing bumper-to-bumper eighty miles per hour. J— was driving the beat-up Chevy Blazer with everything we own lashed to the roof or dragging in a trailer behind us. The cat and the dog slept in the back seat, unfazed and uninspired. I watched.

Or riding a gondola at Whistler, outside of Vancouver, just before the winter Olympics. Summer, the ground licked here and there with snow like spilled ice cream. A baby bear ran, and we tried to follow.

Or where Mount Rushmore was sixty-foot heads. Middle of the summer and the air was crystalline, so cold in the morning that we pulled our winter coats from a suitcase in the trailer.

Or the alien formations of the South Dakota Badlands. Earth just like every other planet: eerie and weary and wary of our curiosity. Earth is layer cake and pancake rock layers. And dirigibles strewn like old chew toys. So much ruin to ruin. So much dilapidation unmade, unfurled.

Or in a town with no name, a neon sign flashed, MECHANIC ON DUTY. 7 DAYS in an abandoned garage. The station was surrounded by sagging chain-link and broken beer bottles amidst a haphazard collection of cul-de-sacs and one-story vinyl numbers with front yards of brown grass and cars on blocks. Grass shooting up around the gas pumps. The garage's window glass hanging in shards.

Or a return to my childhood South Carolina, during my divorce—a last-ditch trip to relocate a marriage—where the sad ghost of Alice Flagg haunts the marshes of Pawley's Island searching for her engagement ring. Fourteen years since I'd been here. Streets and parks and tiny plazas now dwarfed by roadside waterslides and beachwear shops with three-story-tall sharks plummeting from roofline to parking lot. We found Wacca Wache Estates off of Wachesaw Road where the Waccamaw people once lived, worked, buried their dead, where in the woods my brother and I hunted bad guys with kitchen knives. The Intracoastal. Found the marshes where I collected oysters for a science fair project to prove their Deuteronomic uncleanness, to prove to my sub-conscious self that the Church wasn't feeding me another strand of imaginary logic. Could I have crossed that bridge every day? Could I have pushed my toddler sister in a stroller around this mall? Was that the shop where we bought my prom dress? Could I have eaten fresh-caught whitefish and flounder at this pier? Are those nurse sharks part of my memory or someone else's? If there are ungraspable memories, these are where they live and where they'll stay—along the threshold of experience.

FROM A WINDOW in my living room, I watch a loggerhead shrike soaked by rain on my fencepost. The shrike looks like a wet blue jay in black-and-white film. A predatory songbird, ultimate contradiction, it swoops down, pecks at the ground, finds a burrowing grub, and flies into a tree. Two more shrikes follow into the tree where, I imagine, they'll have a little snack. Shrikes are known to impale their tiny prey—rodents, lizards, smaller birds, insects—on thorns or the pointy metal protrusions on chain-link fences. They are liked masked robbers, these birds, talonless but clever enough. From my perch, it's a silent bird film. The sliding window, a threshold. This is my first shrike sighting.

[Sooner or later you're going to have to write about this. You're going to have to write this down. You're going to have to see beyond the fog of forgetting and see it, see *it* for *it*. Sooner or later your father's brain is going to stop communicating with his body, tuneless as petrified bone. He's going to punch your mother, push her down. He's going to shit in his pants while watching TV. You won't be there to clean up the mess. Your mother will clean up the mess with the last vestiges of her frazzle. She hates messes. She's always hated messes. But this is not the mess one bargains for; it's part of a deal nobody bargains for.]

IN HIS MEMOIR *Planetwalker,* activist John Francis describes how in 1983 he swore off motorized vehicles. Soon after that, tired of arguing with people about environmental issues, he went silent and began walking across America. He remained silent for seventeen years, managing to get a PhD along the way without ever saying a word. Instead, Francis listened and discovered that "how we treat each other when we meet each other" is as close to protecting the earth as you can get. Silence breeds witness. And witnesses write down what they see.

[YOUR FATHER WILL wear diapers. He won't wipe himself. Your mother will wipe his ass. He'll forget how to chew his food or swallow his food. He'll bang his head hard against walls. That mechanism in the brain that fires at the speed of light and says, GO to every bodily function will slow, will eventually stop. His internal organs will inflame and shrivel. Liver, pancreas, lungs. Eventually his heart will stop beating, though that's the last to go. He is healthy as an ox in his football player-contractor-tennis player body. You are not proud of this fact; rather you wish he were frail and sickly so he'd die more quickly.]

WHEN I WAS a kid, I practiced being blind, hours and hours with my eyes closed feeling my way around the house and in the yard, down the street. In this new world of Alzheimer's, silence became a practice too. We sat in silence for—was it years? The notion that I might hear something as important as my own voice beyond the noise kept me seeking the void, the black hole, the vortex where nature thrashes about but no voice disturbs, with eyes closed. I dreamed about it, whole vistas without language.

[IN FOUR DAYS your family will move him into a nursing home. Your mother repeats as if a chant that it's a Memory Care Unit in an Assisted Living Facility. Semantics alleviating the deepest guilt. Look at the people in Memory Care. They smile, drool like lobotomized asylum inmates. You're all shipping your father away. This is what it is called. Handing him off. You're all gathering. Siblings, mother, grandmother, uncle, aunt whoever else wants to help, and you're moving your father into a bachelor pad at the local loony bin. You're four days away from this event. Your brother's flying in. Your sister's driving down from college.]

IN HER MEMOIR *When Women Were Birds,* Terry Tempest Williams meditates on the nature of silence, of being silenced. The book's catalyst: shelves of old journals bequeathed to Williams by her mother. When she opens the journals to read them, she discovers that every single one is empty. Her mother never wrote a thing in them. Williams seeks to understand her mother's decision not to fill her journals—and the space that silence creates. She writes, "Silence introduced in a society that worships noise is like the moon exposing the night. Behind the darkness is our fear." In the diminishing light of a back porch, in the falling light, in the light, fragrant jasmine, butterflies, statue of Saint Francis, like twin sadnesses father and daughter listened.

[YOU'RE GIVING HIM back the armoire that was once his, now yours. Now where you keep your clothes. It's going to furnish his new room. From atop this piece of furniture, you stole quarters as a kid. He always had piles of quarters! You're four days away from the rest of his life, a life in which your father lives in a nursing home, and you visit him once or twice a week, and you'll sit with him and the other patients, and you'll laugh and maybe you'll draw pictures or maybe you'll make sculptures of tiny feet. Or maybe, nothing.]

JAMES TATE IN his introduction to 1997's *The Best American Poetry*: "poetry speaks against an essential backdrop of silence." Poetry witnesses the witness. Against this backdrop, Dad asked one day, "What if we could borrow things from God?" Only short bursts of language now. Beyond this, chaos.

[You feel like a psychic who can only see half a future. A sort of Cassandra's curse. You know what it will look like to bring him to the Home, to set him up in his bachelor pad with his single bed and his dresser that you've returned to him and his La-Z-Boy and his clothes in the closet, his family photos, his slate gray adult diapers. No throw rug. Residents trip and fall on them. This bothers you. There will be staff, nurses, curious residents. What you can't see, can't wrap your head around, is what will happen when you have to say goodbye to him in that room. When the locked outer doors open and he can't follow. Will you leave him sitting on the edge of the bed? Will you say, "Bye, Dad. See you later, Dad"? Will you weep? Will he chase after you? Will he hit you? You dream that your father is punching you in the face. Every time he walks into the movie-frame dream, he cocks his arm back and lets a fist fly. Will he do that? Will he feel betrayed? Will he look like a bag of flesh left in a heap in the corner of his tiny loony-bin room? Or will you leave him at a table playing blocks with other residents? Watching TV with his kindreds? Eating dinner in the dining room where the cook serves mashed potatoes and too-soft broccoli, chicken cut into tiny chunks? Will you leave him while he's napping? You and your family will return to the family house without him— you'll have to. You will speak very little; it will feel as though you've just come inside from a subarctic trek, like your bodies are unclenching. You'll want to melt into the floor. You'll tiptoe around each other. Mother, grandmother, sister, brother, you. You'll all have the urge to spring your father from jail. You'll feel jumpy, watching the TV at a screaming volume, and you'll want to retrieve him from his new life somewhere else. He belongs with you! You'll want to carry him in your arms, you'll want to bring him back to vibrancy like a baby into the world. You'll want to suckle him. You'll want his old brain in a jar on the windowsill like a memento of a bygone surgery, you'll want to replace his brain with a perfect brain. You'll want to dress him like you would a child for his first day of school. You'll want, you'll want.]

IN HIS POEM "Always," Mark Strand's Great Forgetters sit around a dimly lit table—a demented poker club—gradually and calmly eliminating everything known from the face of the earth until all that's left is "the blaze of promise everywhere." Simultaneously a poem about redemption and a kind of horror show unmasking nightmares of the apocalypse—I think of barren landscapes and desperate souls running from zombies or foraging for the last edible plant on the planet or watching Cormac McCarthyesque baby-roasting-on-a-spit scenarios—seldom do we witness the brain's apocalypse as a sign the world's ending from the inside, a story in which forgetting becomes its own final atomic bomb. Is the hope of resurrection, rebirth, revision the legitimate hope of a blank mind, the final ambition of escape from one's own destruction? What if scientists could regenerate the brain cells of an obliterated brain—after all its memories have sloshed away—so that a blank-slate body, a more perfect Frankenstein's monster, might start over in a literal bath of born again? We'd be empty vessels creating new synaptic selves every day.

Neuroscientist Joshua Greene calls brain science the soul's last stand. Once we figure out the brain's myriad secrets, he figures, there will be no more arguing for the soul because the soul is housed in our brain matter. When you watch a person with Alzheimer's, you see it—once the brain starts to sour, a self becomes a ghost playing hide-and-seek—or you see the alternative, a soul trapped in a deflated brain-and-body. Trapped souls are the stuff of horror, too, less like a light going out and more like a poltergeist making the lights flicker on and off. I don't know where I fall in the argument for a soul. I'm inclined to love creation myths, destruction myths, explanation myths because they tell us something about our nature. The idea that I would be transfixed by a myth of a flaming rock mid-ocean says something about my capacity for wonder, though it does little to explain to me the birth of human existence. Maybe it's enough to believe that we're all born out of the same eternal moment, and we'll all die in that same eternal moment. Or maybe it's not quite enough.

From across the world, my ex muses, "Your brain's an organ. Your mind's the space surrounding it—the locus of the metaphysical shit." But if you lose your brain, if your brain atrophies, or you get knocked out by a three-hundred-pound linebacker, or you start hoarding the wrong proteins, well, fuck, you lose your God, your ghosts, your poetry. You just lose it. Worse, you lose the safety of not knowing. The eloquence of imperfection. You're here in this room, and then you're bursting particles and light.

To forget: to fail to remember, to put out of one's mind; cease to think of or consider. To forget oneself: to act improperly or unbecomingly. Forgetting makes us unknow our selves because our selves are conglomerations of our experiences, and forgetting is an act of unfastening. An Alice-in-Wonderland-feast of unbirthdays. Knowledge is not secure. In "At the Fishhouses" Elizabeth Bishop imagines the acquisition of knowledge to be painful: "If you tasted it, it would first taste bitter, / then briny, then surely burn your tongue," and mutable, "derived from the rocky breasts / forever, flowing and drawn, and since / our knowledge is historical, flowing, and flown." Knowledge is an ancient bird, a trickster raven, or a set of collected data, a memory as it changes instant to instant. Bishop's mother-ocean is the roiling mess of what's inside. To leave behind the ancient *gnarus* is to lose the acquaintance of both joy and pain.

Ryan and I paddled the heavy canoe between mangroves. Usually we spotted lightning whelks, needlefish, mullet, the manatee family that lived nearby, an osprey with a striped, wriggling sheepshead in its talons. But the day we left Dad, we didn't see anything alive. Fiddler crabs and mullet had been replaced by huge swaths of blooming carpet algae. We sat in the canoe like figurines, wondering where everything living had gone when Ryan's phone rang, a nurse at the home relaying the message that Dad had punched a hole through a shatterproof glass window. Kendal screamed to us from the house. They got the call too. We paddled home. We moved quickly.

[YOUR FATHER WILL sleep in a room coated in urine, where he's peed in corners, on slippers, into picture frames, on the windowsill all through the night. Where are you? Your father will sleep in a room splattered in shit and piss and drool stains. When you see him, his fingernails will be soiled with shit. Where? He will sleep alone and wake up to strangers. He will hurt himself and others. Day after day, each face an unfamiliar one, even yours, even ours. His head will change shape because he rams into walls headfirst. God, all the drooling. His neck bent at a forever right angle. His eyes simultaneously unrecognizing and tormented. He will stop eating. He will crouch beneath a table. You will all mourn periodically, forever. You're tired of telling this story, tired of facing the photographic image of time spent. Dad, where have you gone? You will go to sleep and wake tomorrow a rememberer. You will wander the rooms of your house and shuffle these pages. You're going to sleep now to wake up tomorrow, and again, and again. Where are you? Where are you? You are here. You will sleep on your father's leather couch, won't you, one more time? Right here. You are everywhere, as pollen, as dirt. Close your eyes and listen. Still no final word. No definitive mythology-cosmology-architecture-structure. The world unpeels its tangerine layers, and you see with new eyes, you hear with infant ears. No last word. Still. Witness. Witness. You don't mind.]

IN THE ANCIENT worldview, a static earth is bound by an outer sphere containing all the stars. When Copernicus stationed the sun at the center of everything, he set earth rotating on its own axis. He sent us spinning into the void as not a lone prisoner but as a sister. Others—Galileo then Kepler—followed suit with angles and math, elegant proofs and slide shows of the moon. Today, black holes loom on our horizons, into which whole universes pour like milk sliding from a microscopically angled slab. From the anuses of black holes, white holes, and once the white holes fill up: the end of life as we know it, the hope of new life, new Big Bangs, new thieves in the night, new creationists, new heavens and earths. Invisible parallel universes can be proven, scientists say, by serious equations, yearslong equations, equations that wrap and loop around the globe. Or elegant, discrete equations, answers so simple that scientists become the gods of our age.

HE LISTENED TO the mangrove darkness one night while still at home, head cocked. He said under his breath, one, two, three times, "There's something out there." Somewhere in the struggle between word and deed is a cosmology that includes losing and finding, capture and release, genesis and fall. His cosmology appeared in a delicate watercolor painting from one of our Wednesday sessions. On an outer space of cheap canvas, a blue dancer is birthed in a spout from a pink planet, and bending away from the wind, pieces of the dancer's body fly off in splotches like a stop-motion video of sand dune erosion. The dancer's arms raise to ether, one leg kicked into the air, one leg planted firmly on the pink planet's orb. The planet cradles intimations of life in blue squiggles of algae birthed from the mouth of a storm, white patches of cloud, and purple snaking rivers. The dancer's arc follows the curve of the planets around it, with which it shares space, and faces a purple planet inlaid with darker purple corkscrews, flanked by twelve purple and blue moons. Some moons are paired, others stand alone in a neat row.

In Dad's cosmology, the dancer's god, an outline of earth's oceans gone wild, our planet—a father's and a daughter's—sharding and shattering in the wind. A trickster working her magic. A dancer fixing his universe into graspable concentric circles. Birth superimposed onto chaos. There he is, see him?

PHOTOGRAPH

Strictly speaking, one never understands anything from a photograph.

—Sontag

A MAN.
A girl.
A pool.
Some light.

POSTSCRIPT

I'M IN BED with Mom the day after he dies. Sleeping in his spot. Spooning Mom because what else can I do but hold her body close? The TV is on, and she curls toward it like an unfurling fern. In and out of sleep we catch snippets of *Law and Order*. We cry intermittently. There is no vision of a man in white. No bursting into flames. Darkness and TV glow envelop us. We're two women bound by grief. Whatever story we imagine later will be our collective memorabilia folder, tucked into a drawer, sometimes hard to look at, sometimes filled with his contagious laughter.

ACKNOWLEDGMENTS

Deepest gratitude to everyone at Kore Press for championing this book. I'm honored to be part of the Kore family. Special thanks to my editor, Ann Dernier, who took on the dual roles of generous and patient editor and pandemic cheerleader—both of which I sorely needed—and to Shanna Compton, who not only designed this book, but with whom I've been blessed to work with on almost thirty picture and young adult titles.

Thank you to the editors of *Lumen Magazine* and *Tarpaulin Sky* for first publishing versions of "Photograph" and "A Language You Have Yet to Discover." Some of the lines in this book also appear in "Cytokinesis" a poem from my first book.

Thank you to the editors of the following presses in whose contests this manuscript was a finalist for their time and consideration: Cleveland State Poetry Center, Graywolf Press, Pleiades Press, Subito Press, Tarpaulin Sky Press.

This manuscript won a 2013/2014 literary arts grant from the Arts and Cultural Alliance of Sarasota County, which included a residency at the Hermitage Artists Retreat—a few miles from where Dad and I loved to go for walks—where I completed a solid draft. Thanks for the time and support.

Deepest thanks to Sarah Leavitt, John Skoyles, and Daniel Tobin for their most kind words.

This book owes its life to my mentors. I stand on your shoulders, and my love of many of the texts cited here can be traced to you. Thanks to Josh for following me back across country to take care of my dad all those years ago. I'll never forget that kindness. Thank you to family and friends who listened to me hem and haw for many years over this book. Rick, thanks for your unwavering belief in me.

Finally, but always first in my book, thank you and deepest love to Aaron and the boys for being my home.

CITED MATERIAL, GHOSTS, INFLUENCES, AND INSPIRATIONS

Ammons, A. R., *A. R. Ammons Selected Poems*. Lehman, David, ed. New York: The Library of America, 2006.

Atwood, Margaret. *True Stories*. New York: Simon and Schuster, 1981.

Bachelard, Gaston. *The Poetics of Space*. Boston: Beacon Press, 1994.

Bender, Aimee. *The Girl in the Flammable Skirt*. New York: Anchor Books, 1999.

Bierhorst, John, ed. *The Red Swan: Myths and Tales of the American Indians*. Albuquerque: University of New Mexico Press, 1992.

Bishop, Elizabeth. *The Complete Poems: 1927–1979*. New York: Farrar, Straus and Giroux, 1979.

Borges, Jorge Luis. *The Book of Imaginary Beings*. New York: Viking, 2005.

Campbell, Joseph. *Thou Art That: Transforming Religious Metaphor*. Novato, Calif.: New World Library, 2001.

Childcraft. Vol. 2. Chicago: Field Enterprises Educational Corporation, 1960.

Crick, Francis. *The Astonishing Hypothesis: The Scientific Search for the Soul*. New York: Scribner, 1994.

Didion, Joan. *The White Album*. New York: Farrar, Straus and Giroux, 2009.

DiFranco, Ani. *Dilate*. Righteous Babe Records, 1996. Album.

Dobyns, Stephen. "Approaching Subject Matter," *Next Word, Better Word*. New York: Palgrave Macmillan, 2011.

Duane, Daniel. *Caught Inside: A Surfer's Year on the California Coast*. New York: North Point Press, 1996.

Emerson, Ralph Waldo. *The Spiritual Emerson: Essential Works by Ralph Waldo Emerson*. New York: Penguin, 2008.

Francis, John. *Planetwalker*. Washington DC: National Geographic, 2008.

García Lorca, Federico. *In Search of Duende*. New York: New Directions Publishing Corporation, 1998.

Goethe, Johan Wolfgang von. *Truth and Poetry: From My Own Life*. Translated by John Oxenford. London: Bell & Daldy, 1871. [Accessed on Kindle]

Greene, Joshua. "Social Neuroscience and the Soul's Last Stand." http://www.joshua-greene.net/publications/social-neuroscience-and-the-souls-last-stand-pdf.

Keats, John. *Keats: Poems and Selected Letters*. York, Bantam Books, 1962.

Kelly, Brigit Pegeen. *Song*. Brockport, New York: BOA Editions, 1995.

Komunyakaa, Yusef. *Pleasure Dome: New and Collected Poems*. Middletown, Connecticut: Wesleyan University Press, 2001.

Kübler-Ross, Elizabeth. *On Death and Dying*. New York: Scribner Classics, 1997.

LeDoux, Joseph. *Synaptic Self*. New York: Penguin Books, 2002.

Lehman, David, ed. *The Best American Poetry 1997*. New York: Scribner, 1997.

Levy, Andrew. *A Brain Wider Than the Sky: A Migraine Diary*. New York: Simon & Schuster, 2009.

Lopez, Barry. *Vintage Lopez*. New York: Vintage, 2004.

Maurer, Konrad and Ulrike Maurer. *Alzheimer: The Life of a Physician and the Career of a Disease*. Translated by Neil Levi with Alistair Burns. New York: Columbia University Press, 2003.

Mazur, Gail. *Figures in a Landscape*. Chicago: The University of Chicago Press, 2011.

The New King James Bible. Nashville: Thomas Nelson Publishers, 1988.

Orr, Gregory. *Poetry as Survival*. Athens: University of Georgia Press, c2002.

Plath, Sylvia. *Ariel*. New York: Perennial Classics, 1999

Pollan, Michael. *The Botany of Desire*. New York: Random House, 2001

Rilke, Rainer Maria. *Book of Hours: Love Poems to God*. New York, Riverhead, 2005.

Sacks, Oliver. *Migraine*. New York: Vintage Books, 1999.

Shermer, Michael. "Why People Believe in Weird Things." TedTalk, 2006.

Sontag, Susan. *On Photography*. New York: Farrar, Straus and Giroux, 1977.

Shelley, Mary. Letter to Maria Gisborne, August 15, 1822. Accessed at Project Gutenberg from *The Life and Letters of Mary Wollstonecraft Shelley, Vol. II* by Florence A Thomas Marshall.

Steinbeck, John. *East of Eden*. New York: Penguin Books, 2002.

Strand, Mark. *The Continuous Life*. New York: Alfred A. Knopf, 1999.

Swensen, Cole. *Gravesend*. Berkeley: University of California Press, 2012.

Williams, Terry Tempest. *When Women Were Birds: Fifty-four Variations on Voice*. New York: Farrar, Straus and Giroux, 2012.

Winterson, Jeannette. *Art Objects: Essays on Ecstasy and Effrontery*. New York: Vintage International, 1997.

Young, Gary; Buckley, Christopher. *The Geography of Home: California's Poetry of Place*. (Charles Wright's introduction to his poems). United States: Heyday Books in conjunction with the Clapperstick Institute, 1999.

See the full-color artwork on the author's page at KorePress.org.

Photo credit: R. J. Hooker

ALEXIS ORGERA is also the author of two poetry collections, *How Like Foreign Objects* and *Dust Jacket*. Her writing has appeared or is forthcoming in various literary journals including *Bennington Review*, *Black Warrior Review*, *Carolina Quarterly*, *Chattahoochee Review*, *Conduit*, *Denver Quarterly*, *Gulf Coast*, *Hotel Amerika*, the *Journal*, *jubilat*, *Memorious*, *New South*, *Prairie Schooner*, the *Rumpus*, *storySouth*, *Tarpaulin Sky*, *Third Coast*, *Vinyl*, and elsewhere. She is a freelance editor and cofounder of Penny Candy Books and Penelope Editions, an indie picture book press and young adult imprint that encourage big conversations and reflect diverse realities (and imaginations). In addition to wordplay, she is a visual artist and studies/practices the art of growing plants for food, medicine, and connection.

More at alexisorgera.com.

COLOPHON

Head Case comes to you, dear reader, by the dedicated in-house and out-of-house team at Kore Press Institute. KPI is currently housed in (but has not occupied since early March, 2020) Room 201 of the Dunbar Pavilion—an African American Arts and Culture Center named after the poet Paul Laurence Dunbar, and Tucson's first and only segregated school for African-Americans up until 1952. We acknowledge where we live and work is on occupied Tohono O'odham and Yaqui ancestral lands.

From the time *Head Case* was chosen by the editorial team at KPI, our industrious staff included Lisa Bowden, Ann Dernier, Tina Howard, Casely Coan, Morgan Vega, Rosalie Morales Kearns, Rylee Carrillo-Waggoner, and our editorial crew was made up of the following poets and writers: Debra Gregerman, Tracie Morris, Leticia Del Toro, July Westhale and Estella Gonzalez. Gratitude to our book designer Shanna Compton. And appreciations for Georgie—the wonder dog who kept things calm in the KPI studio and at home.

We wish to acknowledge all our family members who made room for our work at home, at the kitchen table, with the light on all night, with internet interruptions, with power outages and fires raging, with smoke filled skies, supply scarcities, soaring infection rates, and unbearable losses. We hold you close, more than ever, with deep gratitude for your expansive hearts.

Kore (kor-ay) is Greek for *daughter* and another name for the mythic Persephone—the goddess taken into the underworld who wrestled with darkness (and its enticements, sexiness, and fraught, lonely trade-offs). She reemerged periodically above ground only after her mother and Hades struck a deal over how to share their beloved. Kore's appearance above ground inspired the change in season: from winter to spring, fallow to fruit, dark to light, struggle to innovation. The Kore/Persephone myth has taken on intense meaning during this time of global pandemic where we wait in fallow, in an "underworld life," for a little more light to come lead us to a new place.

At the time of publication, we are all living this more intensely than ever.

Our goal the last twenty-eight years at Kore Press Institute has been to collectively effort toward building more just and radically connected communities with creative, innovative, and intersectional works that amplify and celebrate all women's voices, especially the most marginalized.

You can support one of the country's oldest feminist, literary publishers by buying books directly from Kore or at an Indie bookseller near you. Become a sustaining member of the Press and learn about KPI's award-winning programs by visiting korepress.org.